Source Readings in Music History

Books by Oliver Strunk

Source Readings in Music History

Essays on Music in The Western World

Essays on Music in The Byzantine World

SOURCE READINGS IN
MUSIC HISTORY

The Classic Era

Selected and Annotated by
OLIVER STRUNK

W · W · NORTON & COMPANY
New York · London

Musical examples by Gordon Mapes

ISBN   0   393   09683   1

To the Memory of
CARL ENGEL
1883–1944

ACKNOWLEDGMENTS

THE EDITOR wishes to acknowledge with thanks the co-operation of J. M. Dent & Sons, Ltd., London, who have granted permission to reprint the translation, by Eric Blom, of Gluck's dedication to *Alceste* from a work copyrighted by them. Acknowledgment is due also to Harvey Olnick for his excellent notes on Grimm, Rousseau, and Grétry.

Throughout the book, small letters refer to notes by the authors of the individual selections, arabic numerals to editor's notes. The abbreviation "*S.R.*" followed by a Roman numeral refers to another volume in the *Source Readings in Music History*.

Contents

I

THE TRANSITION TO THE MUSICAL PRACTICE OF THE CLASSICAL PERIOD

II

OPERATIC RIVALRY IN FRANCE: THE "QUERELLE DES BOUFFONS"

III

CRITICAL VIEWS OF ITALIAN OPERA: ALGAROTTI AND GLUCK

IV

THE EUROPEAN SCENE

Preface to the Five-Volume Edition

My *Source Readings in Music History*, a music-historical companion running to more than 900 pages and extending from classical antiquity through the romantic era, was originally published in 1950. That it is now being reissued in parts is due to a recognition, shared by the publishers and myself, that the usefulness of the book would be considerably enhanced if the readings for the single periods were also available separately and in a handier form. From the first, the aim had been to do justice to every age without giving to any a disproportionate share of the space. Thus the book has lent itself naturally to a division into parts, approximately equal in length, each part complete in itself. For use in the classroom, the advantages of the present edition are sufficiently obvious. For the casual reader, whose interest in the history of music is not likely to be all-inclusive, it will have other advantages, equally obvious. In the meantime, the original edition in one volume will remain in print and will be preferred by those who wish to have the whole between two covers, to be able to refer readily from one part of the book to another, and to be able to consult a single index.

In reprinting here the foreword to the edition of 1950, I have retained only those paragraphs that apply in some measure to all parts of the whole.

O. S.

Rome, 1965

Foreword

THIS BOOK began as an attempt to carry out a suggestion made in 1929 by Carl Engel in his *Views and Reviews*—to fulfil his wish for "a living record of musical personalities, events, conditions, tastes . . . a history of music faithfully and entirely carved from contemporary accounts." It owes something, too, to the well-known compilations of Kinsky and Schering and rather more, perhaps, to Andrea della Corte's *Antologia della storia della musica* and to an evaluation of this, its first model, by Alfred Einstein.

In its present form, however, it is neither the book that Engel asked for nor a literary anthology precisely comparable to the pictorial and musical ones of Kinsky and Schering, still less an English version of its Italian predecessor, with which it no longer has much in common. It departs from Engel's ideal scheme in that it has, at bottom, a practical purpose—to make conveniently accessible to the teacher or student of the history of music those things which he must eventually read. Historical documents being what they are, it inevitably lacks the seemingly unbroken continuity of Kinsky and Schering; at the same time, and for the same reason, it contains far more that is unique and irreplaceable than either of these. Unlike della Corte's book it restricts itself to historical documents as such, excluding the writing of present-day historians; aside from this, it naturally includes more translations, fewer original documents, and while recognizing that the somewhat limited scope of the *Antologia* was wholly appropriate in a book on music addressed to Italian readers, it seeks to take a broader view.

That, at certain moments in its development, music has been a subject of widespread and lively contemporary interest, calling forth a flood of documentation, while at other moments, perhaps not less critical, the records are either silent or unrevealing—this is in no way remarkable, for it is inherent in the very nature of music, of letters, and of history. The beginnings of the classical symphony and string quartet passed virtually unnoticed as developments without interest for the literary man; the beginnings of the opera and cantata, developments which concerned him immediately and deeply, were heralded and reviewed in documents so numerous that, even in a book of this size, it has been possible to include only the most significant. Thus, as already suggested, a documentary history of music cannot properly exhibit even the degree of continuity that is possible for an iconographic one or a collection of musical monuments, still less the degree expected of an interpretation. For this reason, too, I have rejected the simple chronological arrangement as inappropriate and misleading and have preferred to allow the documents to arrange themselves naturally under the various topics chronologically ordered in the Table of Contents and the book itself, some of these admirably precise, others perhaps rather too inclusive. As Engel shrewdly anticipated, the frieze has turned out to be incomplete, and I have left the gaps unfilled, as he wished.

For much the same reason, I have not sought to give the book a spurious unity by imposing upon it a particular point of view. At one time it is the musician himself who has the most revealing thing to say; at another time he lets someone else do the talking for him. And even when the musician speaks it is not always the composer who speaks most clearly; sometimes it is the theorist, at other times the performer. If this means that few readers will find the book uniformly interesting, it ought also to mean that "the changing patterns of life," as Engel called them, will be the more fully and the more faithfully reflected.

It was never my intention to compile a musical Bartlett, and I have accordingly sought, wherever possible, to include the complete text of the selection chosen, or—failing this—the complete text of a continuous, self-contained, and independently intelligible passage or series of passages, with or without regard for the chapter divisions of the original. But in a few cases I have made cuts to eliminate digressions or to avoid needless repetitions of things equally well said by earlier writers; in other cases the excessive length and involved construction of the original has forced me to abridge, reducing the scale of the whole while retaining the essential continuity of the argument. All cuts are clearly indicated, either by a row of dots or in annotations.

Without the lively encouragement and patient sympathy of the late William Warder Norton my work on this book would never have been begun. Nor is it at all likely that I would ever have finished it without the active collaboration of my father, William Strunk, Jr., Emeritus Professor of English at Cornell University, whose expert assistance and sound advice were constantly at my disposal during the earlier stages of its preparation and who continued to follow my work on it with the keenest interest until 1946, the year of his death. A considerable number of the translations now published for the first time are largely his work and there are few to which he did not make some improving contribution.

My warmest thanks are due to Professor Otto Kinkeldey, of Cornell University, and to Professor Alfred Einstein, of Smith College, for their extraordinary kindness in consenting to read the entire book in proof and for the many indispensable corrections and suggestions that they have sent me; again to Alfred Einstein, and to Paul Hindemith, for a number of constructive recommendations which grew out of their experiments with sections of the manuscript in connection with their teaching; likewise to my old friends Paul Lang, Arthur Mendel, and Erich Hertzmann, who have always been ready to listen and to advise.

Acknowledgment is due, also, to Dr. Dragan Plamenac, who prepared the greater number of the brief biographical notes which accompany the single readings; to two of my students—Philip Keppler, Jr., who relieved me of some part of the proofreading and J. W. Kerman, who prepared the index; to Gordon Mapes, for his careful work on the autographing of the musical examples; and to Miss Katherine Barnard, Miss Florence Williams, and the entire staff of W. W. Norton & Co., Inc., for their unflagging interest and innumerable kindnesses.

OLIVER STRUNK

The American Academy in Rome

I

The Transition to the Musical
Practice of the Classical Period

1. J. J. Quantz

This outstanding flute player and composer for the flute began his career as an oboist in the Dresden royal orchestra in 1718. Quantz was born in 1697 and received his first training in counterpoint under Zelenka and Fux at Vienna. In 1724 he set out on a series of extended journeys: he visited Italy and studied in Rome with Gasparini and went in 1726 to Paris, where he stayed seven months and published several instrumental works, and to London, where he stayed three months. In 1728 Quantz entered into relations with Frederick the Great, who became a great admirer of his art and engaged him in 1741 as a flutist and composer to his court. He retained this position until his death in 1773.

Quantz was an extremely prolific composer: for the King alone he wrote three hundred concertos and two hundred other compositions. His best-known work, however, and the one that best testifies to the solidity of his musicianship, is his method for the flute, *Versuch einer Anweisung die Flöte traversière zu spielen* (1752). The book does not confine itself to flute playing but discusses questions of general importance for the musical practice and musical aesthetics of the time.

From the Versuch einer Anweisung die Flöte traversière zu spielen [1]

[1752]

HOW A PERFORMER AND A PIECE OF MUSIC OUGHT TO BE JUDGED

1. THERE IS perhaps no art so subject to every man's judgment as music. It would seem as though there were nothing easier than to judge it. Not only every musician, but also everyone who gives himself out as a musical amateur, wishes likewise to be regarded as a judge of what he hears.

---

1 Text: The original edition (Berlin, 1752), pp. 275–281, 293–308, 323–325, 328–329, 331–334.

2. We are not always satisfied that each performer whom we hear should be at pains to offer what lies within his powers; we often expect to hear more than we ourselves have ever been used to hearing. If, in a company, not all sing or play with equal perfection, we often attribute all the excellence to one performer, considering the others as of no account, without reflecting that one may have his merits in this style, another in that, one, for example, in Adagio, another in Allegro. We fail to consider that the attraction of music consists, not in equality or similarity, but in variety. If it were possible for all musicians to sing or play with the same ability and in the same taste, as a result of this lack of an agreeable variety the greater part of our enjoyment in music would be lost.

3. We are seldom guided by our own impression, which would after all be the surest guide, but we are at once anxious to hear which one is the ablest of those who are singing or playing, just as though we could at one time oversee and estimate the skill of several persons, like things that only show their worth and merit on the scales. And now we listen only to him who is in this fashion pronounced the ablest. A piece which he performs carelessly enough, often intentionally, and which is into the bargain a very poor one, is puffed up as a marvel; to another, for all the great industry with which he is at pains to perform some choice piece, we grant barely a few moments' attention.

4. We seldom allow a performer time enough to show his strength or weakness. We also fail to consider that a performer is not always in a position to offer what he understands; that often the slightest accident may easily cause him to lose all his self-possession; and that, as a result of this, we ought in fairness to hear him more than once before venturing to pass judgment on him. Some performers are forward and have perhaps a few pieces in which they can show everything that they can do and, so to speak, unburden themselves of their whole art at one time, so that we hear them once and for all. Others who are not thus forward and whose art cannot, as in the former case, be confined to a few pieces have not the same advantage. For most listeners are only too inclined to be hasty in their judgments and allow themselves to be altogether too much prepossessed by what they hear at first. Had they the patience and the opportunity to hear each performer several times, no great insight would be required as a rule; they would need only to be guided by their own feelings, without prejudice, and to see which performer gave them the most pleasure in the long run.

5. As regards composition, we are no better off. We are unwilling to be regarded as ignorant; at the same time we feel, no doubt, that we may

not always be competent to make a proper decision. Hence we are usually inclined to begin by asking who the composer is, in order to be guided by this in our judgment. Does the piece prove to be by someone to whom we have conceded our approval in advance, it is at once unhesitatingly pronounced beautiful. Does the contrary apply, or have we perhaps some objection to the author's person, the whole piece passes for worthless. Anyone who wishes to convince himself of this in a positive way need only publish two pieces of equal excellence under different names, one of which is in favor, the other out of favor. The ignorance of many judges will surely soon betray itself.

6. More modest listeners, who do not credit themselves with sufficient insight to judge a thing, often have recourse to a musician, whose word they accept as irrefutable truth. Assuredly, by listening to many good performances and to the judgment which experienced, instructed, and honest musicians pass on them, we can attain a certain degree of knowledge, especially when we ask also about the reasons why a piece is good or bad. This, then, ought to be one of the most reliable means of avoiding error. But are all those who make music their business at the same time musical experts or musical scholars? Have not ever so many of these learned their art as a mere trade? It can then easily happen that we address our questions to the wrong person and that the musician, quite as much as the amateur, is swayed in his decision by ignorance, envy, prejudice, or flattery. Like wildfire, such a verdict spreads abroad at once and so takes in the uninformed who rely on a supposed oracle of this kind that in the end there arises from it a prejudice which is not easily again removed. What is more, it is not even possible for every musician to be a competent judge of all that can occur in music. Singing requires its special insight. The variety of the instruments is so great that the powers and the lifetime of a single person would be insufficient for attaining insight into all their properties. Before placing his trust in the judgment of a musician, the musical amateur must therefore accurately determine whether his musician is really in a position to judge correctly. With one who has thoroughly mastered his art, we are on safer ground than with one who has only followed his good instincts; the latter, however, is also not to be entirely rejected. And because it is not easy for anyone to be so free from the passions that his judgments do not sometimes even run counter to his knowledge, the musical amateur must also in this respect accept the judgment of a musician with caution. There are some whom almost nothing pleases but what they have written themselves. Alas, then, for all music that has not the honor to thank their celebrated pens for its

existence! Whenever, to avoid scandal, they find themselves obliged to praise a thing, do they not do so in a way which, after all, betrays that to praise is difficult for them? Others, just the other way, praise everything indiscriminately, to fall out with nobody and to make themselves agreeable to everyone. Many a rising young musician regards nothing as beautiful but what has flowed from his master's inventive genius. Many a composer seeks his reputation in unrelieved remote modulations, obscure melodies, and other things of this sort. With him, everything is to be extraordinary and unusual. No doubt he has won applause by his real merits and also surreptitiously gained a following by other means. Does anyone expect him and those who blindly honor him to pronounce a thing beautiful which does not agree with this way of thinking? The older generation complains of the melodic extravagances of the younger; the younger generation makes fun of the dry style of the older. Nevertheless, we occasionally find musicians who grasp a thing impartially according to its real worth, who praise what ought to be praised, and who reject what ought to be rejected. Such musical scholars are the safest to trust. Yet the upright and able musician must be very much on his guard lest his passions lead him to commit some injustice and especially lest professional jealousy deceive him, for his judgment, to be sure, while it can be the most correct, can also, because of the reputation he enjoys, be the most dangerous.

7. Now since music is the sort of art which must be judged, not according to our own fancy, but, like the other fine arts, according to good taste, acquired through certain rules and refined by much experience and exercise; since he who wishes to judge another ought to understand at least as much as the other, if not more; since these qualities are seldom met with in those who occupy themselves with the judging of music; since, on the contrary, the greater part of these are governed by ignorance, prejudice, and passions which hinder correct judgment; many a one would do much better if he would keep his judgment to himself and listen with greater attention, if, without judging, he can still take pleasure in music. When he listens more to judge the performer needlessly than to enjoy the music, he arbitrarily deprives himself of the greater part of the pleasure which he would otherwise take in it. And when, even before the musician has finished his piece, our critic is already occupied in imposing his mistaken opinions on his neighbors, he makes the musician lose, not only his self-possession, but also his power to finish with a stout heart and to demonstrate his ability as he might otherwise have done. For who can remain insensible and self-possessed when, here and there among his listeners, he

sees expressions of disapproval? The hasty judge, moreover, is in constant danger of betraying his ignorance to others who are not of his opinion and perhaps understand more than he does; he can expect, therefore, no advantage from his judgment. From this, we may conclude how really difficult it is to take upon ourselves the office of a music critic and to discharge it honorably.

8. In judging music, besides obeying the usual dictates of reason and fairness, we should always pay particular attention to three points, namely, to the piece itself, to the performer, and to the listener. A fine composition may be mutilated by a bad performance; a poor composition, on the other hand, deprives the performer of his advantage; we must first determine, therefore, whether it is the performer or the composition that is responsible for the good or bad effect. With regard to the listener, as with regard to the performer, much depends on the various constitutions of the temperament. Some prefer the magnificent and lively style, some the mournful and profound, some the gay and delicate; each is governed by his inclinations. Some have considerable knowledge which others lack. We are not always carried away immediately the first time we hear this piece or that. It often happens that a piece pleases us today which tomorrow, if we chance to be in a different mood, we can scarcely sit through; on the other hand, a piece may displease us today in which tomorrow we discover beauties. A piece may be well written and well played; even so it fails to please everyone. A poor piece badly played may displease many; at the same time it finds a few admirers. The place in which a piece of music is performed can put many obstacles in the way of our judging it correctly. We hear, for example, one and the same piece, today from near by, tomorrow from far off. In each case we notice a difference. We may hear a piece intended for a vast place and a large orchestra in its proper setting. It will please us immensely. But if, at some other time, we hear the same piece in a room, performed perhaps by other persons, with a few instruments accompanying, it will have lost half its beauty. A piece that has well-nigh enchanted us in the chamber may be barely recognizable when we hear it in the theater. If, on the one hand, we were to ornament a slow movement, written in the French taste, with many arbitrary embellishments as though it were an Italian Adagio, or if, on the other hand, we were to perform an Italian Adagio in a good, dry, straightforward style with pretty, pleasing trills in the French taste; the former would become wholly unrecognizable—the latter would sound very plain and thin; as a result, neither one would please either the Frenchman or the Italian. Each piece, then, must be played in the style that belongs to it; unless

this is done, there can be no judgment. Supposing, further, that each piece were played, according to the taste proper to it, in these two ways, no Italian could judge the French and no Frenchman the Italian, for both are prepossessed by prejudices in favor of their country and their national music.

9. After this, everyone will grant me, I believe, that the correct and impartial judgment of a piece of music requires, not merely a little insight, but perhaps the highest degree of musical skill; that far more is involved than merely being able to sing or play a little ourselves; and that, as a result of this, if we would judge, we must apply ourselves assiduously to the attainment of that knowledge which reason, good taste, and art have placed within our reach. And further, I hope that no one will wish to dispute my contention that not every one of those who commonly set themselves up as judges of music is equipped with this knowledge and that, for this reason, there must arise a great detriment to music, musicians, and musical amateurs, who are kept thereby in a constant state of uncertainty.

10. I shall attempt to indicate, by means of certain characteristic signs, the chief qualities of the complete performer and of the well-written piece of music, in order that musicians, and musical amateurs as well, may have at least some guidance in forming their judgments and in determining to which performer or to which piece of music they may properly give their approval. Let everyone who seeks to judge try always to do so without prejudice, without passion, with fairness. Let him proceed cautiously and not hurry himself unduly. Let him regard the thing itself and not allow himself to be blinded by secondary considerations which have nothing to do with it; for example, whether the performer or composer is of this or that nationality, whether or not he has traveled abroad, whether he claims to be a pupil of a famous master, whether he is in the service of a great lord, or of a little one, or of no one at all, whether he has a musical character or no character, whether he is friend or foe, young or old, and so forth. In general, we shall not easily be unfair if, instead of saying of a performer or a piece of music, "It is worthless," we say only, "It does not please me." The latter everyone has the right to say, for no one is obliged to be pleased with anything. The former, however, we ought in fairness to leave solely to the real musical experts, who are in any case duty bound to indicate the reasons for their verdict.

.   .   .   .   .

28. To judge an instrumental composition properly, we must have an exact knowledge, not only of the characteristics of each species which may occur in it, but also, as already observed, of the instruments themselves. In itself, a piece may conform both to good taste and to the rules of composition, and hence be well written, but still run counter to the instrument. On the other hand, a piece may conform to the instrument, but be in itself useless. Vocal music has certain advantages which instrumental music must do without. The words and the human voice work to the composer's greatest advantage, with regard both to invention and to characterization. Experience clearly shows this when, in the absence of voices, arias are played on an instrument. Without words and without the human voice, instrumental music, quite as much as vocal music, should express certain passions and transport the listeners from one to another. But if this is to be properly managed, to compensate for the absence of words and of the human voice, neither the composer nor the performer may have a soul of wood.

29. The principal species of instrumental composition in which voices take no part are: the concerto, the overture, the sinfonia, the quartet, the trio, and the solo. In each of the following there are two varieties: the concerto, the trio, and the solo. We have concerti grossi and concerti da camera. The trios are, as the phrase goes, either elaborate or gallant. With the solos the case is the same.

30. The concertos were originated by the Italians. Torelli is said to have written the first ones. A concerto grosso consists in a mixture of various concerted instruments wherein, as an invariable rule, two or more parts—the number may sometimes run as high as eight or even higher—concert with one another. In the concerto da camera, however, there is only a single concerted instrument.

31. The qualities of a concerto grosso require, in each of its movements: (1) a magnificent ritornello at the beginning, which should be more harmonic than melodic, more serious than humorous, and relieved by unisons; (2) a skillful mixture of the imitations in the concerted parts, in order that the ear may be unexpectedly surprised, now by this instrument, now by that; (3) these imitations must be made up of short and pleasing ideas; (4) there must be a constant alternation of the brilliant and the ingratiating; (5) the inner tutti sections must be kept short; (6) the alternations of the concerted instruments must be so distributed that one is not heard too much and another too little; (7) now and then, after a trio, there must be woven in a short solo for one instrument or another; (8) before the end the solo instruments must briefly repeat what they had at

the beginning; and (9) the final tutti must conclude with the loftiest and most magnificent ideas of the first ritornello. Such a concerto requires numerous accompanying players, a large place, a serious performance, and a moderate tempo.

32. Of concertos with a single concerted instrument, the so-called "concerti da camera," there are likewise two varieties. Some, like the concerto grosso, require many accompanying players, others a few. Unless this is observed, neither the one nor the other has its proper effect. From the first ritornello one can gather to which variety a concerto belongs. If this is serious, magnificent, more harmonic than melodic, and relieved by many unisons, the harmony changing, not with eighth or quarter measures, but with half or full measures, many players must accompany. If, on the other hand, it consists in a fleeting, humorous, gay, or singing melody, the harmony changing rapidly, it will have a better effect with a few players accompanying than with many.

33. A serious concerto, that is, a simple one written for many players, requires the following in the first movement: (1) There should be a magnificent ritornello, with all the parts well elaborated. (2) There should be a pleasing and intelligible melody. (3) There should be regular imitations. (4) The best ideas of the ritornello may be broken up and used for relief within or between the solos. (5) The thorough bass should sound well and be suitable for use as a bass. (6) The composer should write no more inner parts than the principal part permits, for it is often more effective to double the principal melody than to introduce forced inner parts. (7) The progressions of the thorough bass and of the inner parts may neither impede the principal part in its liveliness nor drown out or stifle it. (8) A proportional length must be observed in the ritornello. This should consist of at least two main sections. The second of these, since it is to be repeated at the end of the movement as a conclusion, must be clothed with the finest and most magnificent ideas. (9) Insofar as the opening idea of the ritornello is neither singing nor wholly suitable for solo use, the composer must introduce a new idea, directly contrasted with the first, but so joined to it that it is not evident whether it is introduced from necessity or after due deliberation. (10) The solo sections must be in part singing, while the ingratiating should be in part relieved by brilliant, melodious, harmonious passages, always suited to the instrument, and also, to maintain the fire to the end, by short, lively, magnificent tutti sections. (11) The concerted, or solo, sections may not be too short or the inner tuttis too long. (12) The accompaniment to the solo must contain no progressions which might obscure the concerted part; on the contrary,

it must be made up alternately of many parts and few, in order that the principal part may now and then have room to come to the fore with greater freedom. In general, light and shade must be maintained throughout. When the solo passages permit it, or when the composer knows how to discover such as will, it is most effective that the accompanying parts should introduce beneath them something familiar from the ritornello. (13) The modulation must always be correct and natural, not touching on any key so remote that it might offend the ear. (14) The laws of meter, to which the composer has at all times to pay strict attention, must here, too, be exactly observed. The caesuras, or divisions of the melody, may not fall on the second or fourth quarter in common duple time, or on the third or fifth measure in triple. The composer must endeavor to maintain the meter with which he begins, whether it be by whole or half measures or, in triple time, by two-, four-, or eight-measure phrases; otherwise the most artful composition becomes defective. In triple time, in an arioso, if the melody permits frequent divisions, successive caesuras after three- and two-measure phrases are permitted. (15) The composer may not follow up the solo passages with uniform transpositions *ad nauseam;* on the contrary, he must imperceptibly interrupt and shorten them at the right time. (16) The ending may not be hurried unduly or bitten off too short; on the contrary, the composer should endeavor to make it thoroughly solid. Nor may he conclude with wholly new ideas; on the contrary, the last solo section must repeat the most pleasing of those ideas that have been heard before. (17) The last tutti, finally, must conclude the Allegro, as briefly as possible, with the second section of the first ritornello.

34. Not every variety of measure is suitable for the first movement of a magnificent concerto. If the movement is to be lively, the composer may employ common duple time, in which the smallest note is the sixteenth, permitting the caesura to fall on the second half of the measure. If it is likewise to be magnificent, he should choose a longer meter, one in which the caesura regularly occupies the full measure and falls only on the down beat. If, however, it is to be both serious and magnificent, he may choose for it, in common duple time, a moderate tempo in which the smallest note is the thirty-second, the caesura falling on the second half of the measure. The dotted sixteenths will in this case contribute much to the magnificence of the ritornello. The movement may be defined by the word *allegretto.* Notes of this kind can also be written in the moderate alla breve time. It is only necessary to change the eighths to quarters, the sixteenths to eighths, and the thirty-seconds to sixteenths. In this case, however, the caesura may always fall on the beginning of the measure. The ordinary

alla breve time, in which the smallest note is the eighth, is to be regarded as the equivalent of two-four time and is more suited to the last movement than to the first, for, unless one writes continually in the strict style, using all the voices, it is more expressive of the pleasing than of the magnificent. In general, triple time is little used for the first movement, unless in the form of three-four time with occasional sixteenths and a movement in eighths in the inner and lowest parts, the harmony changing, as a rule, only with full measures.

35. The Adagio must be distinguished from the first Allegro in every respect—in its musical rhyme-structure, its meter, and its key. If the Allegro is in one of the major keys, for example in C major, the Adagio may, as one prefers, be in C minor, E minor, A minor, F major, G major, or even G minor. If, on the other hand, the first Allegro is in one of the minor keys, for example in C minor, the Adagio may be in E-flat major, F minor, G minor, or A-flat major. These successions of keys are the most natural. The ear is never offended by them, and the same relationships apply to all keys, whatever they may be called. He who wishes to surprise the listener in a painful and disagreeable way is at liberty to choose, beyond these keys, such as may give pleasure to him alone. To say the least, considerable caution is necessary in this regard.

36. For the arousing and subsequent stilling of the passions the Adagio offers greater opportunity than the Allegro. In former times it was for the most part written in a plain dry style, more harmonic than melodic. The composers left to the performers what had been expected of them, namely, to make the melody singable, but this could not be well accomplished without considerable addition of embellishments. In other words, it was in those days much easier to write an Adagio than to play one. Now, as it may be readily imagined that such an Adagio did not always have the good fortune to fall into skillful hands, and since the performance was seldom as successful as the author might have wished, there has come of this evil some good, namely, that composers have for some time past begun to make their Adagios more singing. By this means the composer has more honor and the performer less of a puzzle; moreover, the Adagio itself can no longer be distorted or mutilated in such a variety of ways as was formerly often the case.

37. But since the Adagio does not usually find as many admirers as the Allegro among the musically uninstructed, the composer must endeavor in every possible way to make it pleasing even to those listeners without musical experience. To this end, he should above all strictly observe the following rules. (1) He must aim studiously at the greatest

possible brevity, both in the ritornellos and in the solo sections. (2) The ritornello must be melodious, harmonious, and expressive. (3) The principal part must have a melody which, though it permits some addition of embellishments, may still please without it. (4) The melody of the principal part must alternate with the tutti sections used between for relief. (5) This melody must be just as touching and expressive as though there were words below it. (6) From time to time something from the ritornello must be introduced. (7) The composer may not wander off into too many keys, for this is the greatest impediment to brevity. (8) The accompaniment beneath the solo must be rather more plain than figured, in order that the principal part may not be prevented from making ornaments and may retain complete freedom to introduce, judiciously and reasonably, many or few embellishments. (9) The composer, finally, must endeavor to characterize the Adagio with some epithet clearly expressing the passion contained therein, in order that the required tempo may be readily determined.

38. The final Allegro of a concerto must be very different from the first movement, not only in its style and nature, but also in its meter. The last Allegro must be just as humorous and gay as the first is serious. To this end, the following meters will prove useful: 2/4, 3/4, 3/8, 6/8, 9/8, and 12/8. In no case should all three movements of a concerto be written in the same meter. But if the first movement is in duple time and the second in triple, the last may be written either in triple or in two-four time. In no case, however, may it stand in common duple time, for this would be too serious and hence as little suited to the last movement as two-four or a rapid triple time to the first. Similarly, all three movements may not begin on the same step, but, if the upper part begins in the first movement on the keynote, it may begin in the second on the third and in the third on the fifth. And although the last movement is in the key of the first, the composer, to avoid similarity in the modulations, must still be careful not to pass through the same succession of keys in the last movement as he did in the first.

39. Generally speaking, in the last movement (1) The ritornello must be short, gay, fiery, but at the same time somewhat playful. (2) The principal part must have a simple melody, pleasing and fleeting. (3) The solo passages should be easy, in order that the rapidity of the movement may not be impeded. They may, further, bear no similarity to those in the first movement. For example, if those in the first movement are made up of broken notes and arpeggios, those in the last movement may be rolling or proceed by step. Or if there are triplets in the first movement,

the passages in the last movement may be made up of even notes, or vice versa. (4) The laws of meter must be observed with the utmost severity. For the shorter and more rapid the variety of measure, the more painful it is if these laws are violated. In ¾ and in rapid ¾, ⅜, and ⁶⁄₈ time, the caesura, then, must always fall on the beginning of every second measure, the principal divisions on the fourth and eighth measures. (5) The accompaniment may not employ too many voices or be overcrowded; on the contrary, it must be made up of such notes as the accompanying parts can produce without undue movement or effort, for the last movement is as a rule played very rapidly.

40. To insure a proportional length, even in a concerto, consult a time-piece. If the first movement takes five minutes, the Adagio five to six, and the last movement three to four, the whole is of the proper length. And it is in general more advantageous if the listeners find a piece rather too short than too long.

41. He who now understands how to make a concerto of this sort will have no difficulty in contriving also a humorous little concerto da camera of the playful kind. It will, then, be unnecessary to discuss this separately.

42. An overture, played before an opera, requires a magnificent beginning, full of gravity, a brilliant, well-elaborated principal section, and a good combination of different instruments, such as flutes, oboes, or horns. Its origin is due to the French. Lully has provided excellent models. Some German composers, however, among them Handel and Telemann, have far surpassed him in this. Indeed, the French fare with their overtures very much as do the Italians with their concertos. Still, in view of their excellent effect, it is a pity that the overtures are not more usual in Germany.

43. The Italian sinfonias, having the same purpose as the overtures, naturally require, as regards magnificence, precisely the same qualities. But since most of them are contrived by composers such as have exercised their genius more in vocal than in instrumental music, we have thus far only a very few sinfonias, perfect in all respects, to use as models. Sometimes it seems as though the composers of opera, in contriving their sinfonias, went about it as do those painters who, in finishing a portrait, use the left-over colors to fill in the sky or the costume. In the meantime it stands to reason, as previously mentioned, that a sinfonia should have some connection with the content of its opera or at least with the first scene of it and not, as frequently occurs, conclude invariably with a gay minuet. I have no wish to set up a standard in this regard, for it is impossible to bring under a single head all the circumstances that may occur at the begin-

ning of an opera. At the same time, I believe that it should be very easy to find a mean. It is admittedly quite unnecessary that the sinfonia before an opera consist always of three movements; could the composer not conclude, perhaps, with the first or second? For example, if the first scene involved heroic or other fiery passions, he might end his sinfonia with the first movement. If mournful or amorous passions occurred in it, he might stop after the second movement. But if the first scene involved no particular passions at all, these appearing only in the course of the opera or at the end, he might close with the third movement. By so doing, he would have an opportunity to arrange each movement in a way suitable to the matter at hand. The sinfonia, moreover, would still retain its usefulness for other purposes.

44. A quartet, that is, a sonata for three concerted instruments and a thorough bass, is the real touchstone of the true contrapuntist, as it is also an affair wherein many a one not properly grounded in his art may come to grief. Its use has never become really common; as a result, it may not even be known to everyone. Indeed, it is to be feared that in the end this kind of music will have to suffer the fate of the lost arts. A good quartet implies: (1) pure four-part writing; (2) a good harmonious melody; (3) short, regular imitations; (4) a judicious combination of the concerted instruments; (5) a proper thorough bass suited for use as a bass; (6) ideas of the sort that are mutually invertible, so that one may build either above or below them, the inner parts maintaining an at least tolerable and not displeasing melodic line; (7) that it must not be obvious whether this part or that one has the advantage; (8) that each part, after a rest, must re-enter, not as inner part, but as principal part and with a pleasing melody (this, however, is to be understood as applying, not to the thorough bass, but only to the three concerted parts); (9) that if there is a fugue, it must be carried out in a masterly and at the same time tasteful fashion in all four parts, observing all the rules. A certain set of six quartets for various instruments, chiefly flute, oboe, and violin, composed quite some time ago by Herr Telemann, may serve as particularly beautiful models of this kind of music.

45. A trio, while it is a task less tedious for the composer than a quartet, nevertheless requires on his part almost the same degree of artistry, if it is in its way to be of the proper sort. Yet it has the advantage that the ideas introduced may be more gallant and pleasing than in the quartet, for there is one concerted part the less. In a trio, then, the composer must follow these rules: (1) He must invent a melody which will tolerate a singing counterpoint. (2) The subjects proposed at the beginning of each

movement may not be too long, especially in the Adagio, for in the imitations which the second part makes at the fifth, fourth, and unison, an overlong subject can easily become wearisome. (3) No part may propose any subject that the other cannot answer. (4) The imitations must be brief and the passages brilliant. (5) In the repetition of the most pleasing ideas a good order must be maintained. (6) The two principal parts must be so written that the thorough bass below may be natural and sound well. (7) If a fugue is introduced, it must be, as in the quartet, carried out in all the parts, not only correctly, observing all the rules of composition, but also tastefully. The episodes, whether they consist of passages or of other imitations, must be pleasing and brilliant. (8) While progressions of the two principal parts in parallel thirds and sixths are an ornament of the trio, they must not be overdone or run into the ground, but rather interrupted by passages or other imitations. (9) The trio, finally, must be so contrived that one can scarcely guess which of the two parts is the first.

46. To write a solo is today no longer regarded as an art. Almost every instrumentalist occupies himself in this way. If he has no ideas, he helps himself with borrowed ones. If he is lacking in knowledge of the rules of composition, he lets someone else write the bass for him. As a result, our time brings forth, instead of good models, many monstrosities.

47. As a matter of fact, it is by no means so easy to write a good solo. There are composers who understand composition perfectly and are successful in works for many voices, but who write poor solos. On the other hand, there are composers for whom the solos turn out better than the things for many voices. He who succeeds in both is fortunate. Little need as there is to have mastered all the innermost secrets of composition in order to write a good solo, there is as little chance of accomplishing anything reasonable of this kind without having some understanding of harmony.

48. If a solo is to reflect credit on the composer and the performer, then (1) its Adagio must be in itself singing and expressive; (2) the performer must have opportunities to show his judgment, invention, and insight; (3) the delicate must be relieved from time to time by something ingenious; (4) the thorough bass must be a natural one above which one can build easily; (5) no idea may be too often repeated, either in the same key or in a transposition, for not only can this make difficulties for the player, but it can also become tiresome for the listeners; (6) the natural melody must be interrupted occasionally by dissonances, to arouse the passions of the listeners in a suitable manner; (7) the Adagio must not be too long.

49. The first Allegro requires: (1) a flowing, coherent, and somewhat serious melody; (2) well-connected ideas; (3) brilliant passages, well unified melodically; (4) a good order in the repetition of the ideas; (5) choice and beautiful progressions at the end of the first part, so arranged that, in a transposition, they may conclude the second part also; (6) that the first part must be somewhat shorter than the second; (7) that the most brilliant passages must be reserved for the second part; (8) that the thorough bass must be natural, making such progressions as will maintain a continuous liveliness.

50. The second Allegro may be either very gay and rapid, or moderate and aria-like. In this, the composer must be guided by the first movement. If this is serious, the last movement may be gay. But if it is lively and rapid, the last movement may be moderate and aria-like. With regard to variety of measure, what was said of the concertos must also be observed here, lest one movement be like the other. In general, if a solo is to please everyone, it must be so contrived that it affords nourishment to each listener's temperamental inclinations. It must be neither purely cantabile nor purely lively from beginning to end. And just as each movement must be very different from any other, the individual movements must be in themselves good mixtures of pleasing and brilliant ideas. For the most beautiful melody will in the end prove a soporific if it is never relieved, and continuous liveliness and unmitigated difficulty arouse astonishment but do not move particularly. Indeed, such mixtures of contrasted ideas should be the aim, not merely in the solo, but in all kinds of music. If a composer knows how to hit this off properly and thereby to set in motion the passions of his listeners, one may truly say of him that he has attained a high degree of good taste and found, so to speak, the musical philosopher's stone.[2]

51. These, then, are the chief characteristics of the principal species of musical composition—characteristics which must be present in each according to its kind if a connoisseur is to pronounce it good and worthy of applause. Still there will always be left over a number of listeners who are unable to attain that insight into music which is necessary if our characteristic signs of the excellence of a piece are to be remarked in it. Such listeners, then, must confine themselves exclusively to secondary considerations touching, not the performer's person, but the music in general, considerations which can also to a certain extent afford an indication of the excellence of a piece. They will proceed most securely if, when music

---

2 Cf. Burney's characterization of John Christian Bach (*A General History of Music*, IV, 483): "Bach seems to have been the first composer who observed the law of contrast as a principle. Before his time, contrast there frequently was, in the works of others, but it seems to have been accidental. Bach, in his symphonies and other instrumental pieces, as well as his songs, seldom failed, after a rapid and noisy passage, to introduce one that was slow and soothing."

is sung or played at great assemblies (these, however, should be such assemblies as convene for no other purpose than to hear music—assemblies at which music is not regarded as a mere side issue and at which the listeners are made up both of connoisseurs and of the musically uninstructed), they will observe the expressions and gestures of the audience, endeavoring to determine: whether only a few or the majority of the company are aroused to attention; whether one listener or another gives signs of pleasure or displeasure; whether the performers are approached or ignored; whether there is silence or loud conversation; whether anyone nods his head in time to the music; whether anyone is desirous of knowing the author of the piece; whether the company, when the piece is over, shows a wish to hear it again. Finally, they must also inquire a little into their own feelings and determine whether the music they have heard has moved them, even though they cannot always give the reason for this. Then, if all the favorable considerations just enumerated are found in a piece of music, even the musically uninstructed listener may confidently conclude that it has been well written and well performed.

52. The divergence in taste which asserts itself in all the various nations that take any pleasure at all in art has the greatest influence on musical judgment, not only as regards essential matters, but still more as regards accidental ones. It is therefore necessary to inquire in still greater detail into this divergence, although, as the need arose, I have already commented on it to some extent at various points in the foregoing.

53. Every nation, unless it belongs among the barbarous, has in its music some one quality which pleases it pre-eminently and above others; at the same time this quality diverges in some cases so little from others and is in other cases of so little consequence that we cannot consider it worthy of special attention. In recent times, however, two nations have not only acquired special merit through their improvement of musical taste, but have also, in following their innate temperamental inclinations, come to diverge pre-eminently from one another in this respect. These nations are the Italian and the French. Other nations have most applauded the tastes of these two peoples and have endeavored to imitate one taste or the other and to adopt some part of it. As a result of this, the two peoples before mentioned have been seduced, as it were, into setting themselves up as arbiters of good taste in music, and, since for some time past no foreigner has objected, for several centuries they have actually been, so to speak, the musical lawgivers. From them, good taste in music was brought afterwards to other peoples.

54. Not to go back to its remotest origins, music, like the other fine

arts, was handed down in olden times from the Greeks to the Romans, and, after the decline of Roman splendor, it lay for a long time as though in the dust of oblivion; this much is certain. But which nation it was that first began to rescue music from its decline and to restore it in its renewed form is a question that has been much disputed. We may presume, however, that a really thorough and proper investigation would render a decision in favor of the Italians. To be sure, it took a long time to bring music to that approximation of perfection in which it stands today. It is possible that, at certain times, one nation was somewhat further advanced in this respect and that, at certain other times, another nation came to the fore, only to follow again later on. Charlemagne, at the time he was in Rome, already awarded the palm to the Italian musicians for their singing and even caused a number of them to come to his court. He endeavored to organize his music after Italian models.

55. There is good reason to believe that, long after the time of Charlemagne, the music of the Italians and the French was by no means as different as it is today. Lully—whom the French regard as almost a general in music, continuing to this day to approve his taste throughout all France, endeavoring indeed, whenever any of their countrymen wish to depart from it, to restore it with care and to maintain it, unaltered, in full sway— Lully, as is well known, was an Italian. I will admit that this celebrated man, having come to France very young, adapted himself, to some extent, to the older French music and adopted its taste. But no one will be able to show that it was possible for him to deny altogether the taste peculiar to his own nation, some notion of which he must have gathered in Italy after all. Since Lully's death, however, the taste in music has in Italy been constantly and very noticeably changing, as everyone knows, while in France it has remained precisely the same; for this reason, the divergence between the two has in the meantime really begun to show itself.

· · · · ·

76. If, after this, we wished to characterize in brief the Italian and the French music and to draw a parallel between the divergent tastes of the one and the other, regarding each from its best side, the comparison would run, in my opinion, substantially to this effect:

The Italians, in composition, are broad-minded, magnificent, lively, expressive, profound, lofty in their way of thinking, somewhat bizarre, free, forward, audacious, extravagant, occasionally careless in their meter; at the same time, they are also singing, ingratiating, delicate, moving, and rich in invention. They write more for the connoisseur than for the amateur. The French, in composition, are lively, expressive, natural, pleasing and intelligible to the public, and more correct in their meter than the Italians; at the same time, they are neither profound nor bold but on the contrary very narrow-minded, servile, always the same, commonplace in their way of thinking, dry in invention; they continually warm over the ideas of their predecessors and write more for the amateur than for the connoisseur.

The Italian way of singing is profound and artful, at once moving and astonishing; it engages the musical understanding and is pleasing, charming, expressive, rich in taste and stylish delivery; it transports the listener in an agreeable way from one passion to another. The French way of singing is simple rather than artful, speaking rather than singing, exaggerated rather than natural in expressing the passions and in voice, wanting in taste and stylish delivery, and always the same; it is more for amateurs than for musical experts, better suited to drinking songs than to serious arias, and, while it amuses the senses, it leaves the musical understanding wholly disengaged.

The Italian way of playing is arbitrary, extravagant, artificial, obscure, likewise frequently audacious and bizarre, difficult in performance; it permits a considerable addition of embellishments and requires a fair knowledge of harmony; in the uninstructed it arouses less pleasure than astonishment. The French way of playing is servile but modest, clear, neat and pure in its delivery, easy to imitate, neither profound nor obscure, but intelligible to every man and suited to the amateur; it requires little knowledge of harmony, for the embellishments are for the most part prescribed by the composer; at the same time, it is, for the musical expert, little conducive to reflection.

In a word, the Italian music is arbitrary and the French narrowminded; for this reason, the good effect depends, in the latter case, more on the composition than on the performance, in the former case, almost as much—indeed, in some pieces even more—on the performance than on the composition.

The Italian way of singing is preferable to their way of playing, the French way of playing preferable to their way of singing.

77. The qualities of these two kinds of music might easily be developed at greater length and more thoroughly examined. This, however, would be more suited to a separate and special treatise than to my present purpose. As it is, I have endeavored to enumerate in brief their principal truths and characteristic signs, as also their differences. I leave each of my readers at liberty to draw, from what has been said, his own conclu-

sions as to which taste properly deserves the preference. I am confident that my readers, in fairness to me, will be that much the less inclined to accuse me of partiality in this, since whatever degree of taste I may have acquired myself has flowed both from the Italian and from the French, since I have traveled in both countries with the express purpose of profiting in each from its good side, and since I am therefore an eye- and ear-witness of both kinds of music.

78. Now, if we were to make a thorough examination of the music of the Germans of more than a century ago, we should find that, even that far back, they had reached a very high point, not only in correct harmonic composition, but also in the playing of many instruments. Of good taste, however, and of beautiful melody we should find little trace, save for a few old chorales; on the contrary, we should find their taste and melody alike longer than their neighbors', rather plain, dry, thin, and simple.

79. In composition they were, as indicated, harmonious and many-voiced, but not melodious or charming.

Their writing was more artful than intelligible or pleasing, more for the eye than for the ear.

The very oldest introduced in their elaborate pieces too many superfluous cadences in succession and were accustomed scarcely to modulate from one key to another without first making a cadence, a straightforward procedure with which the ear was seldom surprised.

Their ideas were not well chosen or well connected.

To arouse and still the passions was something unknown to them.

. . . . .

82. However wretched the taste of German composers, singers, and instrumentalists may have been in former times, for all their thorough insight into harmony, it has now taken on, little by little, a very different appearance. For, if we cannot precisely say of the Germans that they have produced a taste of their own, wholly different from the music of other nations, they are the more capable of adopting one from outside, whichever they please, and they know how to profit by the good side of foreign music, whatever its kind.

83. As long ago as the middle of the last century a few celebrated men, some of whom had themselves visited Italy and France with profit, others of whom had taken the works and taste of distinguished foreigners as their models, began to work on the improvement of musical taste. The players of the organ and clavier, among the latter especially Froberger and after him Pachelbel, among the former Reincken, Buxtehude, Bruhns, and

several others, wrote almost as the first the most tasteful pieces of their time for their instruments. Above all, the art of playing the organ, for the most part taken over from the Netherlanders, was carried at this time to a very high point by those just named and a few other skillful men. More recently, this art was brought to its highest and final perfection by Johann Sebastian Bach, a man worthy of admiration. It is only to be hoped, in view of the small number of those who still take a certain pains with it, that with his death this art may not again tend toward decline, or even toward its downfall.

．　．　．　．　．

86. The Italians were formerly accustomed to call the German taste in music *un gusto barbaro*—"a barbarous taste." But now that it has come to pass that several German composers have been in Italy, where they have had opportunities to perform works of theirs with success, both operas and instrumental music, and since at the present time the operas which the Italians find most tasteful, and rightly so, are actually the productions of a German pen,[3] the prejudice has gradually been removed. It must be said, however, that the Germans are indebted—deeply to the Italians and somewhat to the French—for this favorable change in their taste. Every-one knows that, for more than a century, Italian and French composers, singers, and instrumentalists have been in service and have performed operas at various German courts—at Vienna, Dresden, Berlin, Hanover, Munich, Ansbach, and many others. Everyone knows that great lords have sent many of their musicians to Italy and France and that, as I have said before, many of the improvers of German taste have visited one or both of these countries. These have adopted the taste of the one or the other and have hit upon a mixture which has enabled them to write and to perform with success, not only German, but also Italian, French, and English operas and other Singspiele, each in its own language and taste. We cannot say as much of the Italian composers or of the French. It is not that they lacked the necessary talent, but rather that they gave themselves little pains to learn foreign languages and that they could not persuade themselves that, apart from them and without their language, respectable accomplishment in vocal music was still a possibility.

87. When we know how to select with due discrimination from the musical tastes of various peoples what is best in each, there arises a mixed taste which, without overstepping the bounds of modesty, may very well be called the German taste, not only because the Germans were the first

---

3 That of Johann Adolf Hasse.

to hit upon it, but also because, introduced many years ago in various parts of Germany, it still flourishes there, displeasing neither in Italy, nor France, nor any other country.

88. Now, provided the German nation does not again abandon this taste; if it will endeavor, as its most celebrated composers did in the past, to explore it further and further; if its composers of the new generation will apply themselves, as their predecessors did, more diligently than is unfortunately the case at present to mastering thoroughly, along with their mixed taste, the rules of composition; if, instead of stopping at mere melody and at the contriving of theatrical arias alone, they will exercise themselves also in the church style and in instrumental music; if, for the disposition of their pieces and the reasonable connecting and combining of their ideas, they will take as their models such composers as have received general applause, writing in their way and imitating their fine taste—yet not so that they accustom themselves thereby, as so often happens, to dress themselves in borrowed plumage, perhaps copying or warming over the principal section or the whole context from this or that composer; if, far from doing this, they will bend their own inventive faculties to show and clarify their talents without prejudice to others and to become composers instead of forever remaining mere copyists; if the German instrumentalists will refuse to permit themselves to be led astray by a bizarre and comic style, as we have called the Italian, but will take as their models the style of those who sing well and play with a reasonable taste; if finally the Italians and the French will imitate the Germans in their mixture of tastes as the Germans have imitated them; if, as I say, all these things are observed with one accord—then, in time, there may be introduced a general good taste in music. And this is something not at all improbable, for neither the Italians nor the French—though more the amateurs among them than the musicians themselves—are any longer wholly satisfied with their purely national taste alone, but show for some time past more pleasure in some foreign compositions than in their own.

89. In a taste consisting, like the present German taste, in a mixture of the tastes of various peoples, each nation finds something similar to its own—something, then, with which it cannot be displeased. Considering everything said up to this point about the divergence in taste, the purely Italian must have the preference over the purely French; yet, since the former is not now as thorough as it was, having become audacious and bizarre, and since the latter has remained all too simple, everyone will concede that a mixed taste, composed of what is good in both, must be unfailingly more general and more pleasing. For a music that is accepted

and pronounced good, not by a single country or by a single province or by this or that nation alone, but by many peoples—that is pronounced good, nay, that, for the reasons offered, cannot be pronounced other than good—must be, if based in other respects on reason and sound feeling, beyond all dispute the best.

2. Leopold Mozart

The father of Wolfgang Amadeus, himself an excellent violinist and a respectable composer, was born at Augsburg in 1719. He entered the service of the Prince-Bishop of Salzburg, served as a composer and assistant *maestro di cappella* to the episcopal court, and died at Salzburg in 1787.

Leopold Mozart was a prolific composer and wrote a large quantity of works in the most varied forms of sacred and secular music: masses, motets, symphonies, serenades, concertos, oratorios, operas, etc. His best-known work, however, is probably his method for the violin, *Versuch einer gründlichen Violinschule*, published in the year of Wolfgang's birth (1756), one of the oldest and most solid books of its kind. It is, with Quantz's method for the flute and C. P. E. Bach's method for keyboard instruments, an important source for the study of musical practice in the period immediately preceding the dawning of the classical era.

From the Versuch einer gründlichen Violinschule [1]
[1756]

Chapter Twelve
ON READING MUSIC CORRECTLY AND ON GOOD DELIVERY IN GENERAL

1. EVERYTHING turns on good performance—everyday experience confirms this rule. Many a half-composer is pleased and delighted when he hears his musical Galimathias performed by good players who know how to apply the passion, which he has not even thought about, in its proper place, how to make the greatest possible distinction in the characters, which has never occurred to him, and consequently how, by means of a good delivery, to render the whole wretched scribble tolerable to the ears

---

1 Text: The facsimile reprint of the original edition of 1756 (Vienna, 1922), pp. 252–264. A complete translation, by Editha Knocker, was published by the Oxford University Press in 1948.

of the listeners. But on the other hand, who does not know that the best composition is often so miserably performed that the composer himself has difficulty enough in recognizing his own work?

2. The good delivery of a composition in the present taste is not as simple as those people believe who think they are doing very well if, following their own ideas, they ornament and contort a piece in a truly idiotic fashion and who have no conception whatever of the passion that is supposed to be expressed in it. But who are these people? In the main they are those who, since they can scarcely play in time, even tolerably, begin at once with concertos and solos in order (as they stupidly imagine) to establish themselves as quickly as possible in the company of the virtuosi. Some actually reach such a point that, in a few concertos or solos that they have practiced thoroughly, they play off the most difficult passages with uncommon facility. These they know by heart. But if they are to perform even a few minuets in the cantabile style directed by the composer, they are in no position to do so—indeed one sees this already in the concertos they have studied. For as long as they play an Allegro, things still go well, but as soon as they come to an Adagio, they betray their gross ignorance and their poor judgment in every single measure of the piece. They play without order and without expression; they fail to distinguish the loud and the soft; the embellishments are applied in the wrong places, too thickly crowded and for the most part confused; sometimes, just the other way, the notes are too expressionless and one sees that the player does not know what to do. In such players one can seldom hope any longer for improvement, for of all people they are the most prepossessed in their own favor, and he would incur their highest displeasure who sought, out of the goodness of his heart, to persuade them of their mistakes.

3. To read correctly, as directed, the musical compositions of the good masters and to play each piece in accordance with the passion prevailing in it calls for far more art than to study the most difficult concertos and solos. To do the latter does not require much intelligence. And if the player is adroit enough to figure out the fingering he can learn the most difficult passages by himself, provided he practices them diligently. But to do the former is not as easy as this. For the player has not only to attend closely to every annotation and direction and to play the work as it is set down and not otherwise; he has also to enter into the passion that is to be expressed and to apply and to execute all the runs, the legatos and staccatos, the fortes and pianos, in a word, everything that bears in any way on the tasteful delivery of a piece, observing in this a certain good style that can be learned only by sound judgment through long experience.

4. Let the reader now decide for himself whether, among violinists, the good orchestral player ought not to be prized far more highly than the mere soloist. The soloist can play everything as he pleases and adjust its delivery to his own ideas, even to his own hand; the orchestral player must have the ability to grasp at once and to deliver properly the taste, the ideas, and the expression of different composers. The soloist, to bring things out cleanly, has only to practice at home—others must adapt themselves to him; the orchestral player must read everything at sight—often, indeed, passages such as run counter to the natural arrangement of the measure [a]—he must adapt himself to others. The soloist, if only he has a clean delivery, can in general play his concertos acceptably, even with distinction; the orchestral player, on the other hand, must have a considerable grasp of music in general, of the art of composition, and of differences in characters, nay, he must have a peculiarly versatile talent if he is to fill his office creditably, especially if he is ever to act as the leader of an orchestra. Are there some who believe that, among violinists, one finds more good orchestral players than soloists? They are mistaken. Poor accompanists are admittedly numerous enough, but there are very few good ones, for today everyone wants to be the soloist. But as to what an orchestra consisting entirely of soloists is like, I leave this to those gentlemen composers who have performed their works under such conditions. Few soloists read well, for it is their habit to be continually introducing details of their own invention and to regard themselves alone, paying little regard to others.[b]

5. Thus, until the player can accompany quite well, he must play no solos. He must first know exactly how to execute all the various strokes of the bow; he must understand how to apply the fortes and pianos in the proper place and to the proper degree; he must learn how to distinguish the characters of pieces and how to deliver each passage according to its required and peculiar taste; in a word, before he begins to play solos and concertos, he must be able to read the works of many gifted persons correctly and elegantly. From a painting, one sees at once whether he who has painted it is a master of drawing; in the same way, many a musician would play his solo more intelligently if he had ever learned to

---

a *Contra metrum musicum.* Of this I have already given notice in Chapter 1, Section 2, § 4, note *d*. And I do not know what I am to think when I see an aria, by one of those Italian composers who are so celebrated just now, which runs so counter to the musical meter that one would suppose it made by a pupil.
[In the note *d* to which Mozart refers, it is pointed out that common time ordinarily has two

divisions only and that infractions of this rule are excused only in peasant dances or other unusual melodies.—Ed.]
b But what I say does not at all apply to those great virtuosi who, in addition to being extraordinarily gifted as players of concertos, are also good orchestral players. Such people are really deserving of the highest esteem.

deliver a symphony or trio in accordance with the good taste it required or to accompany an aria with the proper passion and in accordance with the character peculiar to it. I shall endeavor to set down some brief rules which the player can make profitable use of in the performance of a piece of music.

6. The player must of course tune his instrument carefully and exactly to those of his fellows; this he already knows and my mentioning the matter may seem somewhat superfluous. But since even those who wish to pass for first violinists often fail to tune their instruments exactly together, I find it absolutely necessary to mention the matter here, the more so since it is to the first violinist that the rest are supposed to tune. In playing with the organ or harpsichord, these determine the pitch; if neither one is present, the pitch is taken from the wind instruments. Some tune the A-string first, others the D. Both do well, if only they tune carefully and exactly. I would mention only one other point; in a warm room the pitch of the stringed instruments gradually falls, in a cold one it gradually rises.

7. Before beginning to play a piece, the player must thoroughly examine and consider it. He must discover the character, the tempo, and the sort of movement that it requires and must carefully determine whether there is not concealed in it some passage, seemingly unimportant at first sight, which will nonetheless be far from easy to play, demanding a special style of delivery and expression. Then, during the performance itself, he must spare no pains to discover and deliver correctly the passion that the composer has sought to apply and, since the mournful and the merry often alternate, he must be intent on delivering each of these in its own style. In a word, he must play everything in such a way that he will himself be moved by it.[e]

8. From this it follows that the player must pay the strictest attention to the prescribed pianos and fortes and not always be scraping away on one level. Nay, without direction and, as a rule, of himself, he must know how to relieve the soft with the loud and how to apply each of these in its proper place, for, following the familiar expression in painting, this is called light and shade. Notes that are raised by a sharp or natural he ought always to attack somewhat more vigorously, reducing his tone again for the continuation of the melody:

---

e It is bad enough that many a player never gives a thought to what he is doing and simply plays off his music as though in a dream or as though he were actually playing for himself alone. If such a player, at the beginning of a piece, gets a few beats ahead of the tempo, he does not notice it, and I will wager that he would finish the piece several measures before his fellows if his neighbor or the leader himself did not call his attention to it.

pia.   *for.*   *pia.*

In the same way he should differentiate in intensity a note that is momentarily lowered by a flat or natural:

p   *f*   *p*

With half notes that occur among shorter values, the invariable custom is to attack them vigorously and then to diminish the tone again:

fp   *fp*

Indeed, quarters are sometimes also played in just this way:

fp   *fp*   *fp*   *fp*

And this is the expression actually called for by the composer when he marks a note with an *f* or *p*, that is, with a forte or piano. But after the player has vigorously attacked the note, he must not let his bow leave the strings, as some clumsy players do; the stroke must be continued and consequently the tone still heard, though it will gently taper off.[d]

9. The accent,[e] expression, or intensity of the tone will fall as a rule on the strong or initial note that the Italians call the *nota buona*. But there are distinct varieties of these initial or "good" notes. The particularly strong notes are the following: in every measure, the note beginning the first quarter; in the half measure, the first note, or, in ¼ time, the first note of the third quarter; in 6/4 and 6/8 time, the first notes of the first and fourth quarters; in 12/8 time, the first notes of the first, fourth, seventh, and tenth quarters. These, then, are the initial notes on which the maximum intensity of the tone will fall, wherever the composer has indicated no other expression. In the ordinary accompaniments for an aria or concerto, in which as a rule only eighth and sixteenth notes occur, they are

---

d Let the reader look up what I have said about this on p. 44, note *k*. [In this note (Chapter 1, Section 3, § 18), Mozart complains of those who cannot play a half note or even a quarter without dividing it into two parts.—Ed.]

e By the word "accent" I understand here, not the French *port de voix*, which Rousseau tries to explain in his *Méthode pour apprendre à chanter*, p. 56, but a pressure (*expression*) or stress, an emphasis, from the Greek ἐν (in) and φάσις (*apparitio, dictio*).

usually written nowadays as separate notes or are at least marked for a few measures at the beginning with a little stroke:

The player must accordingly continue in this way to attack the first note vigorously until a change occurs.

10. The other "good" notes are those which are always distinguished from the rest by a slightly increased intensity, but to which this increased intensity must be very moderately applied. They are: in alla breve time, the quarters and eighth notes, and, in the so-called half triple time, the quarters; further, in common time and in ⅔ and ¾ time, the eighth and sixteenth notes; finally, in ⅜ and ⅝ time, the sixteenth notes; and so forth. When several notes of this sort follow one after another, slurred two and two, the accent will fall on the first of each two, and this first note will not only be attacked somewhat more vigorously but will also be sustained somewhat longer while the second note will be bound to it, quite gently and quietly and somewhat retarded.[f] It often happens, however, that three, four, and even more such notes are bound together by a slur of this sort. In such a case, the player must attack the first of them somewhat more vigorously and sustain it longer and must bind the rest to it in the same bow, without the slightest stress, by reducing the intensity more and more.[g]

11. From Chapters 6 [2] and 7 the reader has seen how much the melody may be differentiated by the legatos and staccatos. The player, then, must not only pay the strictest attention to such legatos as are written out and indicated, but since in many a composition nothing is indicated at all, he must know how to apply the legato and staccato himself in a tasteful manner and in the proper place. The chapter on the many varieties of bowing, particularly in its second section, will serve to show the player how to go about making such alteration in this as he thinks proper, provided always that it is in keeping with the character of the piece.

12. Today, in certain passages, one finds the skillful composer apply-

---

[f] Let the reader look at the illustration of this in Chapter 7, Section 1, § 3, and in particular let him read § 5 in Chapter 7, Section 2, and look at the musical examples.
[Chapter 7, "On the many different sorts of bowing," deals in Section 1 with notes of equal value and in Section 2 with figures consisting of notes of unequal value.—Ed.]
[g] Let the reader call Chapter 7 to mind from

time to time, especially what was said there in Section 1, § 20.
[The concluding paragraph (§ 20) of Section 1 explains that after mastering the various ways of bowing the examples that have been given, the student must learn to play them with taste and so that their variety is immediately perceptible.—Ed.]

[2] Chapter 6 is entitled "On the so-called triplets."

ing the expression in a quite special, unusual, and unexpected way which would puzzle many if it were not indicated.

For the expression and the intensity of the tone fall here on the last quarter of the measure, and the first quarter of the measure following is to be bound to it very quietly, without being stressed. The player, then, is by no means to distinguish these two notes by a pressure from the bow, but is to play them as though they formed a single half note.[h]

13. In gay pieces, to make the delivery really lively, the accent is usually applied to the highest note. This leads to the stress falling on the last note of the second and fourth quarters in common time and on the end of the second quarter in ¾ time, especially when the piece begins with an upbeat.

But in pieces that are slow and sad, this may not be done, for here the upbeat must be, not detached, but sustained and delivered in a singing style.

14. In ¾ and ⅜ time the accent may also fall on the second quarter.

15. The player will notice that, in the example last given, the dotted quarter (d) in the first measure is slurred to the eighth note (c) that follows. Accordingly, at the dot he must not bear down with his bow, but, as in all other situations of this kind, he must attack the quarter with a moderate intensity, hold out the time of the dot without stress, and very quietly bind the following eighth note to it.[i]

16. In the same way, such notes as these, which would otherwise be divided off according to the measure, must never be divided, nor may their division be indicated by a stress; on the contrary, the player must

h Here too let the reader call to mind § 18 and note k in Chapter 1, Section 3.

[The paragraph in question deals in greater detail with the correct performance of syncopa-

tions like those just described; for Mozart's "Note k," see Note d above.—Ed.]

i I have already drawn attention to this in Chapter 1, Section 3, § 9.

simply attack them and sustain them quietly, exactly as though they stood at the beginning of the quarter.[J] This manner of delivery gives rise to a sort of broken tempo which makes a very strange and agreeable impression, since either the inner voice or the bass seems to separate itself from the upper voice; it has the further effect that in certain passages the fifths do not sound together, but are heard alternately, one after the other. Here, for example, are three voices.

17. Not only in the situation just discussed, but wherever a forte is prescribed, the player must moderate the intensity, not foolishly sawing away, above all in accompanying a concerto. Some people either do not do a thing at all or, in doing it, are certain to exaggerate it. The player must be guided by the passion. Sometimes a note requires a rather vigorous attack, at other times a moderate one, at still other times one that is barely perceptible. The first usually occurs in connection with a sudden expression that all the instruments make together; as a rule, this is indicated by the direction *fp*.

The second occurs in connection with those especially prominent notes that were discussed in §9 of this chapter. The third occurs in connection with all the remaining notes first enumerated in §10; to these the player must apply a barely perceptible stress. For even though he sees many fortes written into the accompaniment of a concerto, he must apply the intensity in moderation and not so exaggerate it that he drowns out the soloist. Quite the other way, such intensity, sparingly and briefly applied, must set off the solo part, give spirit to the melody, help out the soloist, and make easier for him the task of properly characterizing the piece.

18. The player, just as he must pay the strictest attention to the legatos, staccatos, fortes, and pianos required by the expression, must also avoid playing away continually with a dragging heavy bow and must be guided by the passion predominating in each passage. Gay and playful passages

J Let the reader just look at §§ 21, 22, and 23 in Chapter 4, where he will also find examples enough. Here belongs also what was said at the end of Chapter 1, Section 3, § 18, by no means forgetting note *h*.

[The several paragraphs in Chapter 4 deal with various ways of bowing such rhythms as eighth, quarter, eighth, or sixteenth, eighth, sixteenth; for Mozart's references to Chapter 1, see Notes d and h above.—Ed.]

must be distinguished by light short strokes and played off joyously and rapidly, just as pieces that are slow and sad must be delivered with long-drawn strokes, richly and tenderly.

19. As a rule, in accompanying a concerto the player must not sustain the notes but must play them off quickly, and in ⁶⁄₈ and ¹²⁄₈ time, to avoid making the delivery drowsy, must cut off the quarters almost as though they were eighth notes. But let him see to it that the tempo remains steady and that the quarters are more audible than the eighth notes.

20. Many who have no notion of taste are never willing to maintain a steady tempo in accompanying a concerto, but are constantly at pains to yield to the soloist. These are accompanists for bunglers and not for masters. If the player has before him some Italian prima donna who cannot even carry off in the proper tempo what she has learned by heart, or any other fancied virtuoso of this sort, he must admittedly skip over whole half-measures if he is to prevent a public disgrace. But when he accompanies a true virtuoso, one who is worthy of this title, he must not allow himself to be seduced into hesitating or hurrying by the prolongations and anticipations of the notes that the soloist knows how to bring in so skillfully and touchingly, but must at all times continue to play in the same steady tempo. Otherwise what the soloist has sought to build up will be torn down again by his accompanying.[k]

21. Furthermore, if the performance is to be good, the players must pay strict attention to one another and especially to their leader in order that they may not only begin together but may also play throughout in the same tempo and with the same expression. There are certain passages in playing which one easily falls to hurrying.[l] Aside from this, the players must take care to play off the chords quickly and together, the short notes following a dot or a rest of small value somewhat after the beat and

---

k The skillful accompanist, then, must be able to judge his soloist. To a respectable virtuoso he must by no means yield, for to do so would ruin the soloist's *tempo rubato*. But what this "stolen time" is may be more easily demonstrated than described. Has he to do, on the contrary, with a fancied virtuoso? Then, in an Adagio cantabile, he may often sustain an eighth note for half a measure until the soloist comes to himself, as it were,

after his paroxysm, and nothing goes in time, for the soloist plays in the style of a recitative.

l Let the reader just call to mind § 38 in Chapter 4. And in Chapters 6 and 7 I have stressed the importance of a steady tempo more than once.

[Paragraph 38 of Chapter 4 deals with the bowing and correct performance of continuous sixteenths; for Chapters 6 and 7, see Notes f and 2 above.—Ed.]

rapidly.[m] If several notes are to be played as an upbeat or after a short rest, the usual thing is to take them in a down-bow, including the first note of the following quarter in the same stroke. Here the players must pay special attention to one another and not begin too early. This is an example with chords and rests of small value.

22. All that I have set down in this last chapter bears in particular on reading music correctly and in general on the clean and sensible delivery of a well-written piece of music. And all the pains that I have taken in the writing of this book have been directed toward one end: to set the beginner on the right path and to prepare him for the recognition and perception of a good musical taste. So I shall stop here, although I have still many things to say to the musical fraternity. Who knows? I may make bold to enrich the musical world with another book if I see that this my desire to serve the beginner has not been altogether useless.

---

[m] Let the reader look up what I have written in §§ 2 and 3 of Chapter 7, Section 2, also the musical examples given in this connection.

[These two paragraphs deal more explicitly with the correct performance of the short note or notes following a dot.—Ed.]

3. C. P. E. Bach

Johann Sebastian's second son, sometimes called the "Berlin" or "Hamburg" Bach, was born in 1714 at Weimar. In 1738 he moved to Berlin and in 1740 became harpsichordist to Frederick the Great. In 1767 Bach gave up this position to become Telemann's successor as director of church music at Hamburg. He died there in 1788.

As a composer, C. P. E. Bach is the foremost representative of the galant style in German music. Especially remarkable are the innovations he introduced into keyboard music, particularly the sonata. He wrote a great deal for instruments, but also much sacred music (Passions, cantatas, etc.).

His theoretical work, the *Versuch über die wahre Art, das Clavier zu spielen* (in two parts, 1753–1762) has remained to the present day a source of primary importance for the musical practice of the time.

From the Versuch über die wahre Art, das Clavier zu spielen [1]

[*1753*]

OF THE EMBELLISHMENTS IN GENERAL

1. No ONE, perhaps, has ever questioned the necessity of embellishments. We may perceive this from our meeting them everywhere in great abundance. Indeed, when we consider the good they do they are indispensable. They tie the notes together; they enliven them; they give them, when necessary, a special emphasis and weight; they make them pleasing and hence arouse a special attention; they help to clarify their content; whatever its nature, whether sad, gay, or of any other sort we please, they

1 Text: As edited by Walter Niemann from the second (1759) edition of the original (5th ed., Leipzig, 1925), pp. 24–31. A complete translation, by W. J. Mitchell, was published by W. W. Norton & Co., Inc., in 1949.

invariably contribute their share; they provide the correct manner of delivery with a considerable part of its occasion and material; a mediocre composition may be assisted by them, while without them the finest melody must seem empty and monotonous, the clearest content at all times unclear.

2. For all the good embellishments may thus do, they may do equal harm if we choose bad ones or apply them in an unskillful way, apart from their proper place and in excess of their due number.

3. For this reason, those who in their pieces clearly indicate the embellishments that belong to them have always followed a safer procedure than if they had left their things to the discretion of unskilled performers.

4. Also in this respect we must do justice to the French for being unusually careful in the marking of their pieces. In Germany, the greatest masters of our instrument have done the same, and who knows but what the reasonable choice and number of their embellishments may have given the occasion to the French today of no longer burdening, as formerly, almost every note with such an ornament, thereby concealing the necessary clarity and noble simplicity of the melody.

5. From this we see that we must learn to distinguish good embellishments from bad, to perform the good ones correctly, and to apply them in their proper place and in due number.

6. The embellishments lend themselves readily to a division into two classes. To the first I assign those customarily indicated either by certain accepted signs or by a few small notes; to the second may be assigned the rest, which have no signs and are made up of many small notes.

7. Since this second class of embellishments depends especially on musical taste and is hence all too subject to change, since in things for the clavier it is for the most part found written out, and since we can in any case spare it, in view of the sufficient number of the others, I shall treat it only briefly at the end in connection with the cadenzas and shall otherwise concern myself only with those of the first class, inasmuch as these have for some time past, so to speak, belonged to the very nature of clavier-playing and will no doubt always remain the fashion. To these familiar embellishments I shall add a few new ones; I shall explain them and, as far as possible, determine their position; I shall, for convenience' sake, give at the same time their fingering and, where it is noteworthy, the manner of their delivery; I shall illustrate with examples what cannot always be said with sufficient clarity; I shall say what needs to be said about certain incorrect or at least ambiguous signs, so that one may learn to distinguish them from the correct ones, likewise about embellishments to be rejected;

finally I shall refer my readers to the sample pieces, and shall hope, by all these means, to clear away more or less the false notion of the necessity of redundant fancy notes in clavier-playing which here and there has taken root.

8. Regardless of this, everyone who has the skill is at liberty to introduce embellishments more diffuse than ours. He need only take care, in so doing, that this occurs seldom, in the right place, and without doing violence to the passion of the piece. Of himself he will understand that, for example, the depiction of innocence or sadness will tolerate less ornamenting than the other passions. He who in this heeds what is needed may be allowed to have his way, for he skillfully combines, with the singing style of playing his instrument, the elements of surprise and fire in which the instruments have the advantage of the voice and, as a result, knows how to awaken and maintain with constant change a high degree of attention in his listeners. This difference between instrument and voice may be preserved unhesitatingly. He who in other respects bestows on these embellishments the care they need may be unconcerned as to whether what he plays can or cannot be sung.

9. At the same time, an overlavish treatment, even of our sort of embellishments, is to be avoided above all things. Let them be regarded as ornaments which can overload the finest structure, as spices which can spoil the finest food. Many notes, being of no consequence, must be spared them; many notes, sparkling enough in themselves, will likewise not tolerate them, for embellishments would only intensify their weight and artlessness, distinguishing them from others. Failing this, I should commit the same error as the speaker who places an emphatic stress on every word; everything sounds the same and is in consequence unclear.

10. We shall see in what follows that some situations permit more than one sort of embellishment; in such cases, let us take advantage of variation; let us apply, here an ingratiating embellishment, here a sparkling one, and sometimes, for variety's sake, let us use a wholly plain delivery when the notes permit it, without embellishment but in accordance both with the rules of good delivery, to be treated in the next part, and with the true passion.

11. It is difficult to determine the position of each embellishment with absolute precision, for each composer, provided he does no violence to good taste, is at liberty in his inventions to prescribe in most places any embellishment he pleases. In this we are content to instruct our readers by a few well-established rules and examples and by illustrating, in any case, the impossibility of applying particular embellishments; in those

pieces which indicate all embellishments there is no need for concern, while in those which indicate little or nothing the embellishments are customarily supplied in the regular way.

12. Since to this day I can name no one who has anticipated me in this difficult matter and who might have cleared for me this treacherous path, I trust that no one will blame me for believing that, even within certain well-established situations, there may perhaps be still a possibility of exception.

13. And since, to make a reasonable use of this material, he must attend to many small details, the reader should exercise his ear as much as possible by diligent listening to good performances and, the better to understand many things, must have mastered above all the art of thorough bass. Experience has shown that he who has no thorough understanding of harmony is, in applying the embellishments, always fumbling in the dark and that he has to thank mere chance, and never his insight, for the fortunate outcome. To this end, where necessary, I shall always add the bass of the examples.

14. Although the singers and the players of instruments other than ours, if they wish to play their pieces well, can no more do without most of our embellishments than we can ourselves, we players of the clavier have followed the more orderly procedure by giving certain signs to the embellishments, clearly indicating the manner of playing our pieces.

15. By not observing this praiseworthy precaution and by seeking, on the contrary, to indicate all things by few signs, not only has the theory of the embellishments been made sour to players of the clavier and even more so to others, but we have also seen the rise of many ambiguous, indeed false signs which sometimes, even today, cause many pieces to be performed unsuitably. For example, the mordent is in music a necessary and familiar embellishment, yet there are few, apart from players of the clavier, who know its sign. I know of a piece in which, as a result of this, a particular passage has often been ruined. This passage, if it is not to sound untasteful, must be played with a long mordent, something which no one would hit upon without an indication. The necessity of using as its indication a sign known only to players of the clavier, there being no other, has resulted in its being confused with the sign of a trill. We shall see in what follows, from the great difference between these two embellishments, how disagreeable an effect this has had.

16. Since the French are careful in placing the signs of their embellishments, it follows that, in hitherto departing altogether, as we have, unfortunately, from their things and from their way of playing the clavier,

we have at the same time also deviated from the precise indication of our embellishments to such an extent that today these once so familiar signs are already becoming unfamiliar, even to players of the clavier.

17. The notes comprised in the embellishments take their accidentals from the key signature. Nevertheless, we shall see in what follows that there are frequent exceptions to this rule, readily discovered by a practiced ear, caused sometimes by the preceding notes, sometimes by the following ones, and in general by the modulations of a melody into another key.

18. But in order that the reader may also overcome those difficulties that arise on this account, I have found it necessary to retain that practice according to which the accidentals are indicated along with the embellishments in all cases. One will find them in the sample pieces, wherever necessary, now singly, now in pairs.

19. All embellishments must stand in a proportioned relation to the value of their note, to the tempo, and to the content of the piece. Especially in those cases where various sorts of embellishments occur and where the passion is not too restricting, it should be remarked that the more notes an embellishment comprises, the longer the note to which it is applied must be, no matter whether this length arises from the value of the note or from the tempo of the piece. The player must avoid detracting from the brilliance that an embellishment is intended to produce by allowing too much of the value of its note to remain left over; at the same time, he must also avoid occasioning a lack of clarity by performing certain embellishments too quickly, something which occurs mainly when he applies many embellishments or embellishments of many notes to notes of small value.

20. Although we shall see in what follows that the player may sometimes intentionally apply to a long note an embellishment that does not wholly fill out its value, he may not release the last note of such an embellishment until the following note is due, for the chief aim of all embellishments should be to tie the notes together.

21. We see, then, that embellishments are used more in slow and moderate tempi than in rapid ones, more in connection with long notes than with short ones.

22. Whatever needs to be observed regarding the value of the notes, the signs, and the small notes, I shall always include as a part of my explanations. The reader, too, will find the small notes printed in the sample pieces with their actual values.

23. All embellishments indicated by small notes belong to the note that follows; the preceding note, in consequence, never diminishes in

value, while the following note loses as much as is made up by the small notes taken together. This observation is the more necessary in that it is commonly disregarded and in that I have been unable to avoid sometimes detaching certain small notes from their main note in the sample pieces, the space being so crowded with signs for fingering, embellishments, and delivery that it required this.

24. In accordance with this rule, then, these small notes are struck in place of the note that follows, together with the bass or with the other parts. Through them the player slides into the note following; this too is very often disregarded in that he pounces roughly upon the main note after having, in addition to this, unskillfully applied or produced the embellishments associated with the small notes.

25. Our present taste being what it is and the good Italian way of singing having made considerable contribution to it, the player cannot manage with the French embellishments alone; for this reason, I have had to compile my embellishments from more than one nation. To these I have added a few new ones. Apart from this, I believe that the best way of playing the clavier or any other instrument is that which succeeds in skillfully combining what is neat and brilliant in the French taste with what is ingratiating in the Italian way of singing. For this the Germans are particularly well adapted as long as they remain unprejudiced.

26. At the same time, it is possible that a few will not be wholly satisfied with this my choice of embellishments, having perhaps embraced one taste alone; I believe, however, that no one can be a thorough judge of anything in music unless he has heard all kinds and knows how to find what is best in each. What is more, I agree with a certain great man who declared that, while one taste has more good in it than another, there is none the less in every taste some particular thing that is good, no taste being as yet so perfect that it will not still tolerate further additions. By means of such additions and refinements we have reached the point at which we are and shall continue to go on and on. This, however, cannot possibly happen if we work at and, as it were, worship one sort of taste alone; on the contrary, we must know how to profit by whatever is good, wherever it may be found.

27. Therefore, since the embellishments together with the manner of their employment make a considerable contribution to fine taste, the player should be neither so changeable that without further inquiry he accepts at every moment each new embellishment, regardless of its sponsor, nor yet so prejudiced in favor of himself and his own taste that out of vanity he refuses to accept anything new whatever. He should of course

put the new thing to a rigorous test before he adopts it, and it is possible that in time the introduction of unnatural novelties will make good taste as rare as art. At the same time, to keep pace with the fashion, the player should be, if not the first, then not the last to take up new embellishments. Let him not oppose them if they do not always appeal to him at first. New things, attractive as they are occasionally, sometimes seem to us perverse. And this is often evidence of the worth of things which in the long run last longer than those which are overly pleasing in the beginning. These last are as a rule so run into the ground that they soon become nauseating.

28. While most of my examples of embellishments are for the right hand, I by no means deny these graces to the left; on the contrary, I urge every player to exercise each hand alone in all of them, for this brings with it a dexterity and lightness in the production of other notes. We shall see in what follows that certain embellishments also occur often in the bass. Apart from this, the player is obliged to reproduce all imitations to the last detail. In short, the left hand must have exercise in this to manage it skillfully; failing this, it will be better to omit the embellishments, which lose their charm if we perform them badly.

. . . . .

II

Operatic Rivalry in France: The "Querelle des Bouffons"

4. F. W. von Grimm

Born at Ratisbon in 1723, Grimm went in 1747 to Paris, where he soon made the acquaintance of Rousseau, d'Alembert, and Diderot, and became associated with the work on the great *Encyclopédie*. In 1776 he was made minister plenipotentiary for Gotha at Paris, a post he held until 1792, when the Revolution forced him to return to Germany. He died in 1807.

Grimm took an active part in the "Querelle des Bouffons" as one of the first and foremost partisans of the Italian *opera buffa*. One of his earliest contributions to this controversy is the little pamphlet *Le petit prophète de Boehmisch-Broda* (1753), which was a musical fable in a pseudo-Biblical style, with thinly disguised references to the contemporary scene. In the same year, 1753, Grimm began to issue periodical reports (the *Correspondance littéraire, philosophique et critique*), which circulated only in a few manuscript copies, sent to a few of the European princely courts. The *Correspondance* contains valuable material for the history of French opera. On the other hand, Grimm took no interest in instrumental music and devoted not a single word to the important changes that were taking place at his time in this field.

The Little Prophet of Boehmischbroda [1]

[*1753*]

Here are written the twenty-one chapters of the prophecy of Gabriel Joannes Nepomucenus Franciscus de Paula Waldstorch, called Waldstoerchel, native of Boehmischbroda in Bohemia, student of philosophy and moral theology in the Greater College of the Reverend Jesuit Fathers, son of a discreet and honorable person, Eustachius Josephus Wolfgangus Waldstorch, master lutemaker and maker of violins, living in the Judengass of the Old Town at Prague, hard by the Carmelites, at the sign of the Red Violin, and he has written them with his own hand, and he calls them his vision: in Latin, Canticum Cygni Bohemici.

---

1 Text: *Correspondance littéraire, philosophique et critique*, XVI (Paris, 1882), 313–336.

THE THREE MINUETS

AND I was in my garret which I call my chamber, and it was cold, and I had no fire in my stove, for wood was dear.

And I was wrapped in my cloak which once was blue, and which has turned white, seeing that it is worn threadbare.

And I was scraping on my violin to limber my fingers, and I foresaw that the carnival of the coming year would be long.

And the demon of ambition breathed upon my soul, and I said to myself:

Come, let us compose minuets for the ridotto of Prague, and may my glory be in every man's mouth, and be known to all the world and to all Bohemia.

And may they point a finger at me, calling me the Composer of Minuets κατ᾽ ἐξοχὴν, which means above all others.

And may the beauty of my minuets be vaunted both by them that dance them and by them that play them, and may they be played in all the inns during the fair of Jubilate [2] at Leipzig, and may everyone say:

Behold the beautiful minuets of the carnival of Prague! Behold the minuets of Gabriel Joannes Nepomucenus Franciscus de Paula Waldstorch, student of philosophy! Behold the minuets of the great composer! Behold them!

And I abandoned myself to all the chimeras of pride, and I was intoxicated by the fumes of vanity, and I put on my hat aslant.

And I marched with long strides about my garret which I call my chamber, and in the intoxication of my ambitious projects I said:

Ah! how my father will glory in his illustrious son! My mother will bless the womb that has borne me and the breasts that have given me suck!

And I took pleasure in the extravagance of my ideas, and I did not tire of them, and I lifted up my head, which I am not wont to bear very high.

And ambition heated me, even though there was no wood in my stove, and I said:

Ah! how beautiful it is to have loftiness of soul, and what great things the love of glory makes one do!

And I lifted up my mantle which once was blue and which has turned white, seeing that it is worn threadbare, and I took my violin, and I composed on the spot three minuets one after the other, and the second was in a minor key.

---

2 The church festival of the third Sunday after Easter, so called from the first word of the Introit of that day.

And I played them on my violin and they pleased me exceedingly; I played them again and they pleased me even more; and I said: Ah! how fine it is to be an author!

THE VOICE

And suddenly my chamber, which is only a garret, was lighted up with a great light, even though there was but a farthing candle upon my table.

(For I burn a tallow candle when I make music, because I am gay,

And I burn rapeseed oil when I study philosophy, because I am sad.)

And I heard a voice which burst into laughter, and its laughter was louder than the sound of my violin.

And I was annoyed to be thus mocked at, for by nature I dislike mockery.

And the voice which I did not behold said:

Be appeased, for I make a mock of your anger, and by nature you dislike mockery.

And be quickly appeased, and renounce your projects of glory, for I have always confounded them, because they were contrary to mine.

And another will compose the minuets for the carnival of Prague, and your minuets will not be played at the Leipzig fair, because you will not have composed them.

For I have chosen and appointed you among all your comrades to proclaim hard truths to a frivolous and presumptuous people which will mock at you (even though by nature you dislike mockery), because it is untractable and flighty, and which will not believe you, because you will speak the truth.

And I have chosen you for this because I do what I please and because I am accountable to nobody.

And you will compose no minuets, for it is I who tell you so.

THE MARIONETTES

And a hand seized me by the hair of my head, and I felt myself borne through the air, and I was on the way from Thursday until Friday, and I was wrapped in my mantle which once was blue and which has turned white, seeing that it is worn threadbare.

And I arrived in a city of which I had never heard tell until that day, and its name was Paris, and I saw that it was very large and very dirty.

And it was afternoon, and it was the fifth hour of the day, and I found myself in a theatre to which people were thronging.

And my heart leapt with joy, for I love to see fine performances, and even though I am not rich, I think nothing of money when I go to them.

And I said to myself (for I love to talk to myself when I have the time):

Doubtless it is here that they play Tamerlane and Bajazeth [3] with great marionettes, for I found the hall too superb to be only a theatre for Polichinelle.[4]

And I heard the violins tuning up, and I said: Doubtless they will also give serenades, and they will make the little marionettes dance after the great ones have spoken their piece.

For I found the theatre to be large enough for that, and even though bringing out the marionettes might cause some confusion in the wings (for they were very narrow), I judged that as many as six marionettes could dance in the front row and that this ought to be very beautiful.

And although I had seen many booths for marionettes in my day, I knew of none more beautiful, seeing that the decorations were superb and the boxes richly decorated, all with much taste and very clean.

And in all the itinerant theatres of German comedy, I had seen nothing that came near it, even though men play in them and not marionettes.

And even though with us the decorations are more brilliant, because they are oiled with oil and expense is not spared, I found none the less that these would have been more beautiful than ours if they had been oiled as with us.

THE WOODCHOPPER [5]

And while I was saying this to myself (for I love to talk to myself when I have the time), I found that the orchestra had begun to play, without my having noticed it, and they were playing something which they called an overture.

---

3 In the first half of the eighteenth century alone, there are no less than a dozen operas—the most famous are those by Handel and Vivaldi—which treat of the invasion (1402) of the Mongol Empire by the Turkish sultan Bajazet I, and his capture by Tamerlane, the famed descendant of Genghis Khan.

4 The French counterpart of the English Punch and the Italian Pulcinella.

5 A caricature of the time-beater, a man employed by the Opéra solely to mark the beat by striking a heavy stick (sometimes a cane or a thick sheaf of papers) against some solid object. Although not uncommon in other ensemble genres (especially church music), audible time-beating at the opera was rare and roundly condemned; it persisted nevertheless until the last decade of the century. Rousseau, in comparing it with Italian direction of opera from the keyboard, remarked characteristically (1756) in his *Dictionnaire de musique*: "The Paris Opéra is the only theater in Europe where one beats the measure without following it" (cf. the article "Battre la mesure").

Rousseau's copy of "The Little Prophet" is annotated in manuscript by him (cf. Poulet-Malassis, *La Querelle des Bouffons*, Paris, 1876); annotations below attributed to Rousseau are based upon this document. At this point, he suggests in the margin that the "woodchopper" is Rebel, i.e., François Rebel (1701–1775), who was associated with the Opéra from 1733 to 1757, first as leader of the first violins and later as a director and manager. His father Jean Ferry Rebel (1666–1747), an equally famous composer and violinist, and one of the last surviving pupils of Lully, beat the time at the Opéra during the last decade and a half of his life.

And I saw a man who was holding a stick, and I believed that he was going to castigate the bad violins, for I heard many of them, among the others that were good and were not many.

And he made a noise as if he were splitting wood, and I was astonished that he did not dislocate his shoulder, and the vigor of his arm terrified me.

And I reflected (for I love to reflect when I have the time), and I said to myself:

Oh! how talents are misplaced in this world, and how genius displays itself none the less, even if it is out of its right place!

And I said: If that man had been born in my father's house, which is a quarter of a league from the forest of Boehmischbroda in Bohemia, he would make as much as thirty farthings a day, and his family would be rich and honored and his children would live in abundance.

And people would say: Behold the woodchopper of Boehmischbroda, behold him! And his talents would not be wasted, whereas in this booth he cannot earn enough to eat his bread and drink his water.

And I beheld that they called that "beating the time," and although it was beaten most forcibly, the musicians were never together.

And I began to regret the serenades that we sing, we pupils of the Jesuits, in the streets of Prague when night falls, for we keep together and we have no stick.

And the curtain rose, and I saw ropes at the back of the stage, and they were throwing them about;

And I said to myself: Doubtless they will fasten them to the head of Tamerlane, and there will be a great procession of other marionettes after him (for there were many ropes), and he will open the scene that way, and the spectacle will be magnificent.

And I found it wrong that they had not fastened the ropes before raising the curtain, as is done with us, for I have good judgment.

THE BLACK EYES

But not at all. And I saw a shepherd enter,[6] and the people cried: Behold the god of song, behold him! And I saw that I was at the French opera.

And his voice affected and flattered my ears, his laments touched me,

---

6 It was often held that the pastoral scene, providing the customary backdrop for early and middle eighteenth-century French opera, was hardly a "return to nature," but rather an affectation of it.

and he expressed with art everything that he wished, and although he sang slowly he did not bore me, for he had taste and soul.[7]

And I saw his shepherdess enter,[8] and she had great black eyes which she made tender to console him, for he had need of consolation, because he said so.

And her voice was light and brilliant, and its tone rang like silver, and it was as pure as the gold which issues from the furnace, and she sang very well her songs which were not well written, and her throat rounded out what was flat.

And although the music was feeble and poor, it did not seem so when she sang, and I said: Ah! the deceitful hussy! For she had art, and her skill wrought an illusion upon me.

And I said to myself (for I love to talk to myself when I have the time):

Doubtless that shepherd and that shepherdess have enemies who force them to sing in marionette booths to spoil their voices and to make them have weak chests.

For I could smell the odor of oil and tallow which was poisoning me, even though I was born in the forest of Boehmischbroda in Bohemia where the air is thick, and though I have pursued all my studies with the aid of a lamp fed with oil that is not good, for it costs only eight farthings; and I have done well in my studies, for I am a scholar.

And I began to curse the enemies of that shepherd and that shepherdess in the sincerity of my heart, for their voices and their singing caused me pleasure even though their music bored me, and I began to feel pity at their fate; and I continued to curse, for I am malicious when I am angered.

THE SORCERESS

And when my shepherdess, whom I call mine because she pleased me, had consoled my shepherd, whom I call mine because he gave me pleasure, and when they had well caressed each other and had no more to tell each other, they went away.

And I saw a woman come striding in,[9] and she came down to the front of the stage, and she frowned and shook her fists, and I judged that she was in a bad temper.

---

7 Identified at this point by Rousseau as Pierre Jélyotte (1713-1797), the most famous French tenor of his day. Although he sang the traditional French repertoire, his popularity with both French and Italian partisans permitted him to remain aloof from the controversy.

8 Identified by Rousseau as Marie Fel (1713-1794), a soprano whose fame equaled that of the tenor Jélyotte. She was also an intimate friend of Baron Grimm.

9 Identified here by Rousseau as Mlle. Chevalier, or more properly Marie Jeanne Fesch, whose career at the Opéra spanned the years from 1741 to 1765—a singer spoken well of by LaBorde. She sang many leading roles in Rameau's tragedies.

And it seemed to me that she was making threats, and I was annoyed, because I am quick of comprehension and I have a natural dislike of threats, and my neighbor said: No, it is I that she is angry with; and his neighbor said: No, it is I.

And I puzzled my head to find out why she was so furious, for her part was only pathetic, and I saw that it was impossible for me to divine the reason.

And she had in her hand a wand which was mysterious, because the poet had said so, and by means of that wand she could do everything and know everything, except how to sing, which she did not know at all, although she thought she did.

And I heard her utter frightful shrieks, and her veins became swollen and her face became as red as Tyrian purple and her two eyes started from her head, and she filled me with fear.

And I saw that those who sing in the church of St. Apollonia at Vyšehrad,[10] though they are well fed and their thirst is well quenched, could never match their lungs against those of the sorceress, and I said: Ah! why are they not here to hear the sorceress? They would not hold their heads so high, and when we take off our hats to them, we students, they would salute us more affably.

And with her voice, although it was off the pitch, she called up the dead, even though she put the living to flight, and I said to myself: Beyond a doubt, those who are dead and buried in this booth have by nature no ears for music.

And there came on an old man [11] whom the woman with the wand called young (for the poet had said so), although he was past sixty. And he gargled before the public and pretended to sing.

And I felt that this was irreverent, and his gargling continued all the time and his part was done; and I said: Since this man needs so many preliminaries before he can sing, they should say to him: Say your part without singing, for you will say it well; for I am judicious and of good counsel.

And his gargling made me laugh, and when I wished to mock at him, his acting overawed me, and I saw that he was a man worthy of veneration, for he had dignity and nobility and he waved his arms in a way no one could rival.

.   .   .   .   .

---

10 A settlement near Prague, centered about a medieval castle.

11 Claude de Chassé (1698–1786), a bass heard at the Opéra for over thirty years. He was a splendid actor but a poor singer.

And I saw that they called that in France an opera, and I noted it in my tablets to jog my memory.

And I was quite content to see the curtain fall, and I said: Ah! never again shall I see you rise!

And the voice which was my guide began to laugh, and I could tell that it was mocking at me, even though that annoyed me, for by nature I dislike mockery.

And it said to me: You will not depart for the ridotto of Prague, and you will not depart, for that is my design.

And you will spend the night here writing down my wishes which I shall dictate to you, and you will proclaim them to the people which I once cherished and which has become odious to me by the number of times it has deserted me.

.   .   .   .   .

And the voice which had spoken to me became strong, vehement, and pathetic, and I wrote.

HERE BEGINS THE REVELATION

O walls which I have raised with my own hand to be a monument of my glory! O walls once inhabited by a people whom I called my own, because I had chosen them from the beginning to make of them the first people of Europe and to carry their glory and their fame beyond the limits which I have set to the universe!

O city which callest thyself the Great, because thou art immense, and the Glorious, because I have covered thee with my wings; listen, for I am about to speak.

And thou, O Place where they have erected the theatre of the Comédie Française, to whom I have given genius and taste for a possession in common, and to whom I have said: Thou shalt have not thine equal in the universe, and thy glory shall be carried from the East to the West and from the South to the North; listen, for I am about to speak.

And thou, frivolous and haughty theatre, thou who hast arrogated to thyself the title of Academy of Music, although thou art none, and although I have not given thee my permission to do so, listen, for I am about to speak.

O people frivolous and flighty! O people addicted to desertion and abandoned to the madness of your pride and your vanity!

Come, let me reckon with you, I who, if I wish, can reckon you as nothing; come, let me confound you in your own eyes and inscribe your baseness upon your haughty forehead with my own hand, in all the languages of Europe.

THE TRANSMIGRATION

You were festering in the mire of ignorance and barbarism; you were groping in the darkness of superstition and stupidity; your philosophers were without sense and your teachers were idiots. In your schools a barbarous jargon was spoken, and in your theatres mysteries were played. And my heart was moved with pity, and I said to myself: This is a pleasant people; I like its spirit, which is buoyant, and its ways, which are gentle; and I will make it my people, for it is my will, and it shall be the first of peoples, and there shall be no people so pretty.

And its neighbors shall behold its glory, which they shall be unable to attain. And when I have formed it according to my desire, it will amuse me, for it is pleasant and agreeable by nature, and I like to be amused.

And I have rescued your fathers from the nothingness in which they were, and I have brought on the day to enlighten you, and I have implanted in your heart the torch of sciences and letters and arts.

.   .   .   .   .

THE FLORENTINE [12]

And even as I had brought the other arts from Italy to give them all to you, I wished to implant music in your hearts and adapt it myself to the genius of your language.

And I wished to create your musicians and to form them, and to teach them to make music that would satisfy my ear and my heart.

And you have scorned my favors, because I have showered them upon you in abundance.

And in the hardness of your hearts you have created an opera which has wearied me for twenty-four years and which is the laughingstock of Europe to this day.

And in your opinionated extravagance you have erected an Academy of Music, although it is none, which I have never recognized.

And you have chosen a Florentine for your idol without consulting me and although I had not sent him.

---

12 Jean Baptiste Lully (1632–1687), the creator of French opera (more properly the *tragédie lyrique*) and of two of its more important ingredients: the French *ouverture*, and a variety of accompanied recitative especially suited to the French language. Born in Florence, he left his native city as a lad of eleven and a half to come to France.

And because he had received a faint gleam of genius, you have dared to oppose him to me, because in my clemency I had given you my servant Quinault.[13]

And you have believed that his monotony would make me impatient and would force me to abandon you, because I am prompt of action and because you wished to tire me with the number of his works.

And you have shouted in the stupidity of your ignorance: Ah, behold the creator of song! Ah, behold him!

And because, with his poverty of ideas, he has done what he could, you call him a creator to this very day, when he has created nothing, and while the Germans have wearied my ears and made my head split for two hundred years, in their churches and in their vespers, with a kind of singing which you call your own recitative, whereas it is theirs (even though they do not boast of it, because they find it bad), and while in the imbecility of your ideas you believe it to have been invented by the Florentine [14] whom you call M. de Lully [15] to this day.

THE PRECURSOR

And notwithstanding your stubbornness and your opinionated dementia, I have not cast you off in my wrath as you deserved, and I have not delivered you to the contempt of your neighbors.

And I took pity on the childishness of your judgment and the dullness of your ear, and I undertook to lead you back to the right way by the very roads on which you had gone astray in the folly of your heart.

And I undertook to make distasteful to you the monotony of the Florentine and the insipidity of those who have followed him for more than forty years.

And I formed a man [16] for this purpose and I equipped his mind, and I animated him, and I said to him: Have genius; and he had it.

And when it was time I sent him and I said to him: Make yourself master of the stage which they call Academy of Music, although it is none, and purge it of all that bad music which they have had produced by people whom I have never avowed, beginning with the Florentine, whom

---

13 Philippe Quinault (1635-1688) was employed by Lully as his librettist. It was not an equal collaboration; the librettist was obliged to conform to the whims of an autocratic composer. Here it is Lully's music that is under attack, a reversal from the opening years of the century when it was held that poor drama owed its success to Lully's excellent music.

14 The identity of French and German recitative and a denial of the unique form and style of Lully's musical declamation cannot be objec-

tively sustained. The comparison, whether justified or not, certainly reveals the then low esteem of the French avant-garde for German music.

15 Lully consistently avoided the Italian form (Giovanni Battista Lulli) of his name, and Grimm makes the most of the fact that even the "idol" of the supporters of native music is an Italian.

16 Identified at this point by Rousseau as Jean Philippe Rameau (1683-1764), the leading French composer of the time.

they call great, and down to little Mouret,[17] whom they call gay and pleasant.

And you will astonish them with the fire and the force of the harmony which I have put in your head and with the abundance of the ideas with which I have supplied you.

And they will call baroque that which is harmonious, as they call simple that which is flat. And after they have called you a barbarian for fifteen years, they will no longer be able to do without your music, for it will have opened their ears.

And you will have prepared the ways which I have imagined to give a music to that people which is not worthy of my benefits, for you are my servant.

. . . . .

THE EMISSARY [18]

That is why the vanity and insolence of your untractability have reached their limit and I am weary of enduring them.

And in another moment I shall sweep you away, as the south wind sweeps away the dust of the fields, and I shall plunge you again into the mire of barbarism from which I rescued your fathers in the movements of my clemency.

And behold the last miracle which I have resolved to perform, and I shall perform one such as I have never before performed, for I am beginning to despise you, because I no longer esteem you.

And I swear it and I say: Behold the last! And I choose for my emissary my servant Manelli, and I drag him out of the mud and I give him shoes, and I say: Cast off your sabots, and after you have traveled up and down through the provinces of Germany to have bread to eat and water to drink, I shall send you where praise awaits you and where you will do my will.

And I shall set Bourbons at your right and Bourbons at your left, and they will protect you, because I love them and I have given them a taste for beautiful things.[19]

And you will sing in the theatre which they call Academy of Music without my consent and, although it is none, you will force them to applaud you with delight, in spite of their resenting it.

---

17 Jean Joseph Mouret (1682–1738), composer of operas and ballets in the style of Lully.
18 Pierre Manelli, the leading singer of the Italian company. He dropped from sight with the return of the troupe to Italy.

19 A reference to the pro-Italian faction among the nobility; Rousseau cites two of the most prominent: the Duchesse d'Orléans and the Conte de Clermont.

And you will not know what to do with all your glory, and you will exclaim in the modesty of your heart: Not to me, not to me, for there are five hundred better than I in my country, and I am the last of my family.

But I have chosen you on purpose, despite the modesty of your heart, from out the five hundred who are better than you, to humiliate this vain and proud people which I am beginning to despise, because I no longer esteem it.

And you will bring it the music of my servant Pergolesi,[20] whom men to this day call divine, because I caused him to spring fully formed from my brain.

And it will be the time of signs and miracles.

And the philosopher will leave his study and the geometer his calculations and the astronomer his telescope and the chemist his retort and the wit his assemblies and the painter his brush and the sculptor his chisel; only their wives will not wish to go, for they will have no ears, and the boxes will be filled by men.

And they will all come to applaud you, and they will await your fair companion as the lover awaits with impatient heart her whom he loves; and they will be enraptured with joy, and they will lift up their hands toward heaven in the intoxication of their souls.

And they will kiss each other with joy, and stranger will clasp stranger in his arms, and they will congratulate each other on the pleasure they have received.

For I shall have opened their ears, and they will exclaim: Oh! Oh! what music! Oh! Oh! what music!

And after they have heard it for three months, they will no longer be able to endure the slowness and monotony of their singing, which they call recitative and I call plainsong.

And their monologues, which they call touching, will make them yawn; the scenes which they call interesting will weary them, and the scenes which they call gay will put them to sleep.

And a spirit of dizziness will seize them, and they will no longer know what they desire or what they do not desire.

---

20 Giovanni Battista Pergolesi (1710–1736), whose sprightly comic opera *La Serva padrona* (composed, 1733) was the first Paris offering of the Italian company (August 1, 1752). The performance at the Opéra, with an overture by Telemann, and on the same bill with Lully's *Acis et Galatée,* fanned the flames of a conflict already announced by Grimm's earlier polemic, his *Lettre sur Omphale.* The Paris première of *La Serva padrona* was, however, some years earlier (October 4, 1746). That event aroused no controversy although the work was well received; the argumentative French were still debating the merits of Rameau *vs.* Lully.

THE MARVELOUS [21]

O people bewildered in the intoxication of your errors, O people slow to understand, hearken to my voice, as I speak to you for the last time, and perceive the constancy of my warnings.

Banish from your Opéra the tediousness which prevents me from attending. Abandon the prejudices which you have sucked with your mother's milk and with which you still daily quench your thirst.

Deliver me from the childish genre which you call the marvelous, when it is marvelous only to you and to your children; be sincere in your repentance, and I will again stretch out my arms to you and will forget the iniquities of your fathers and your own.

And I will create for you an Opéra agreeing with my taste and my desires, and I shall call it Academy of Music, because it will be one.

And I shall be your inspector, and there will no longer be a woodchopper at the head of your orchestra nor any carpenters to direct your choruses.

And I shall be in your orchestra and I shall animate it, and I shall teach it to feel genius in order to reproduce it with taste, and I shall drive out the bad violins and I shall give you songs in their place.[22]

And I shall give you actors who will sing like my servant Jélyotte and like my servant Fel, and no longer will shrieks be heard in your theatre.

And I shall drive out from your theatre both the demons and the shades, and the fairies and the genii, and all the monsters with which your poets have corrupted it through the power which they have conferred upon wands in fits of their madness, without my consent.

And I shall consecrate your opera, like that of the Italians, to great portrayals of great subjects, and to the passions, and to the depiction of all characters, from the pathetic even to the comic.

And you will amuse yourselves no more making lightnings and thunders and tempests, for I shall teach you to make Meropes and Andromaches and Didos speak.

And I shall be with your poets and with your musicians, and I shall teach your poets to write texts and your musicians to write music.

---

21 "Within the pale of this term came scenic effects, decorations, ballets, *divertissements*, and *machines* [stage apparatus]. The purpose of all this paraphernalia was to create an illusion of splendor and magnificence, fit atmosphere within which the doings of gods and heroes were to be unfolded" (Alfred Richard Oliver, *The Encyclopedists as Critics of Music*, New York, 1948, pp. 47–53). Grimm thus satirizes the emphasis on pageantry and effect at the expense of the drama.

22 To replace violins, however bad, with songs is to imply not only a dearth of songs but a superabundance of orchestral forces as well. The charge that the orchestra is overpowering the singer recurs constantly in operatic criticism.

And I shall give your poets invention and imagination in common, so that they will have no more need of the wand or of spells.

And even as your musicians have written notes down to this day, so they will write music which will be music, and I will put genius in their scores and taste in their accompaniments, and I will deliver these from the weight of the notes with which they burden them, and I shall select them myself.

And I shall teach them to be simple without being flat, and they will no more call that which is monotonous beautiful simplicity. And I shall create your recitative, and I shall teach them to write music which will have character and exact and distinct movement, and which will not be void of expression.

And I shall work with them and my genius shall guide them, and I shall assign boundaries and distinctive character to each species, from the tragedy even to the interlude.

And as I have caused one to be performed by my servant Jélyotte and by my servant Fel, which gave you great pleasure because I had it written as I desired, by a man with whom I do what I please, though he rebels against me, for I govern him in spite of his resenting it, and I have named his interlude the *Devin du village*.[23]

So I shall teach your musicians to write pastorals and comedies and tragedies, and they will no more need to say: This is comic, and that is tragic, for it will clearly appear without their saying so, although they do well to say it today.

And your glory will be resplendent on every side, and I myself will spread it among all nations; you will be called the people above all others, and you will have no equal, and I shall not tire of looking upon you because it will be pleasing to me to see you.

And your genius and your wit and your taste and your graces and your charms and your amiability will make my heart leap for joy, for you shall be my people and there shall be no other like you.

THE TENNIS COURT

And if you do not take advantage of the moment while there is yet time, and of the miracle which I have wrought by the last of my emissaries, Manelli, my servant, to humiliate you for having refused to hear

---

23 Both words and music are by Jean Jacques Rousseau. The Fontainebleau performance for the court (October 18, 1752) was followed by an equally successful public première at the Opéra (March 1, 1753). The prestige of the composer held this amateurish work on the boards of the Opéra throughout the century and led to many performances elsewhere both in the original language and in translations. Among the numerous parodies that it inspired is Favart's *Bastien et Bastienne,* of which Weiskern's German version was set to music by the young Mozart (1768).

those whom I had sent to you in great number, and for having persisted in the willfulness of your false judgments and your childish prejudices;

And if the mission of my servant Manelli, the strangest of the miracles that I have ever wrought, cannot bring you back from your delusions and determine you to consecrate your theatre to good music and to banish from it tediousness and flatness;

And if, before mending your ways, you are waiting, in the vanity of your arrogance, for me to send you five hundred others who are better than he, even though I have no wish to do so;

Behold what I say: I will be avenged upon your strange blindness, and your measure shall be full to overflowing.

And I will make your ear as hard as the horn of the buffalo of the forest, and in your calculations you shall be as fierce as the wild ass of the desert.

And in my wrath I will permit you to hiss the music of my well-beloved Tartini and the playing of my servant Pagin.[24]

And I will prevent you from feeling the genius and the sublimity which I have put into Italian music, and in spite of that you will be unable to hear your own, for it will bore you, as it has bored me for eighty years.

And scales will cover your eyes, and you will drive out my servant Servandoni, and you will send for the decorators of the Pont Notre-Dame.[25]

And your theater, which you call Academy of Music without my consent and although it is none, will be deserted and abandoned, and you will go no more to converse, nor your wives to be seen.

And I will inspire my servant Jélyotte with plans of retirement, and in his place I will give you blacksmiths and locksmiths.

And I shall remove my servant Fel, and I will place her where I please, for I cherish her as the apple of my eye.

And the singing will be out of tune from the rising of the curtain even unto the falling of the curtain. And you will be forced to close your theatre, and its doors will not reopen until it has once more become what it was, namely, a tennis court.

---

24 A reference to an intrigue (1750) at the Concerts Spirituels against André Noël Pagin (1721–1785), a celebrated French violinist and pupil of Tartini. Pagin had championed the violin concertos of his teacher too persistently for the conservative clique. He was so humiliated by the experience as to resolve to play henceforth only in private. Dr. Burney heard him in the course of his Continental travels (1770) and reported very favorably.

25 The Florentine decorator and architect Servandoni (1695–1766), senior decorator at the Opéra from 1728 to 1743, was responsible for the introduction of asymmetrical backdrops at that theater. His bold diagonal lines and remarkable use of perspective gave to the tiny French stage an illusion of depth and space. His influence, obscuring another decorator at the Opéra, the French painter François Boucher, even outlasted his break with the directors of the Académie Royale de Musique. Cf. Jeanne Bouché, "Servandoni" (Gazette des Beaux-Arts, 1910, pp. 121–146).

THE SLAP

And I shall carry my vengeance still further. And I shall confound your proud vanity, in which you boast to your neighbors of the geniuses that I have created among you and of the philosophers that I have sent you; while you abuse them in your heart and while you insult me in their persons.

And I shall remember all your ignoble actions and they shall be before my eyes without ceasing:

From the day when you hissed the *Misanthrope* down to that on which you committed the unpardonable sin, preferring the *Carnaval du Parnasse* to *Zoroastre;* [26]

From the triumph of the *Phèdre* of Pradon over the *Phèdre* of Racine [27] down to the triumph of the Opéra Comique over the Comédie Française. [28]

And I shall take away the theatre of the Comédie Française, and I shall establish it in foreign lands, and you will have it no longer, for you will have reduced the actors to beggary.

And far-off peoples will see the masterpieces of your fathers; and they will see them in their theatres and will admire them without making mention of you; for your glory will be passed, and you will be in relation to your fathers what the Greeks of today are in relation to the ancient ones, that is, a barbarous and stupid people.

·   ·   ·   ·   ·

And coarse and licentious vaudeville [29] will be the delight of your spirit, and you will think it delicious.

And the indecency and the flatness of the dialogue will not shock you. And morality will be outraged with impunity among you, for you will

---

26 *Le Carnaval du Parnasse,* a *ballet heroïque* by Jean Joseph Mondonville (1711–1772), was produced at the Opéra on September 23, 1749, court protection assuring a favorable reception. Rameau's *Zoroastre* followed on December 5. The initial run of the latter work was curtailed by the activities of the partisans of Lully, and the false impression was given that the public preferred the works of Mondonville.

27 A reference to the servile copy of Racine's *Phèdre* by Nicolas Pradon (1632–1698). It was, however, the anti-Racine cabal which caused the failure of Racine's play.

28 What Grimm prophesies in jest turned out to be not far from the truth; by the end of the century the Opéra Comique ranked among the leading Paris theaters. At mid-century it was

still a rude bourgeois enterprise (held at the fairs of Saint Laurent and Saint Germain) whose improvised entertainment was a mixture of song and speech. The Comédie Française was then the reigning seat of spoken French drama, although even at this time the "coarse and licentious vaudeville" (Grimm, see below) was known to have penetrated into that theater.

29 A short satirical poem set to unsophisticated music, or more properly, as in the vaudeville-comedy, a more extended poem or series of such poems given stage presentation. Grimm failed to recognize in the vaudeville-comedy, perhaps the prime ingredient of the then emerging *opéra comique,* the true French counterpart of Italian *opera buffa.*

have none, and you will no longer be conscious of what is good nor of what is evil.

And your philosophers will not enlighten you, and I will prevent them from writing, and the press shall be denied to them.

And they will no longer take pleasure in dwelling among you, for I shall no longer be there.

And the voice was silent.

And I, Gabriel Joannes Nepomucenus Franciscus de Paula Waldstorch, called Waldstoerchel, student of philosophy and moral theology in the Greater College of the Reverend Jesuit Fathers, native of Boehmisch-broda in Bohemia, I wept at the fate of that people, for I am tenderhearted by nature.

And I wished to intercede for it, because I am kindhearted and because I was tired of writing, for I had been writing a long time.

And I was wrong, for the voice was angry, and I received a slap, and my head was knocked against the pillar of the corner which to this day is called the corner on the Queen's side.

And I woke with a start, and I found myself in my garret which I call my chamber, and I found my three minuets, of which the second is in a minor key.

And I took my violin and I played them, and they pleased me as before, and I played them again, and they pleased me even more, and I said: Let us write the others quickly, for there have to be two dozen; and I no longer felt the force of genius, for the thing they call opera was always in my mind, and I wrote many notes, but no minuets at all, and in the bitterness of my heart I cried out: Why did I not finish the two dozen before the Vision?

5. J. J. Rousseau

Jean Jacques Rousseau was born at Geneva in 1712 and died in 1778 near Paris. With his battle cry, "Retournons à la nature," Rousseau exerted a deep and lasting influence on the music of his time. He was not technically trained as a musician, but this did not prevent him from taking a passionate interest in things musical. In the "Querelle des Bouffons" Rousseau fought with Grimm on the side of the partisans of the Italian *opera buffa*. His most important writing in this field is his *Lettre sur la musique française* (1753). Rousseau even tried his hand as composer of a comic opera on a French text in which he attempted to follow the principles of the *opera buffa*. The work—*Le Devin du village* (1752)—was extremely successful and played an important role in forming the style of French *opéra comique*. Rousseau was also the author of a valuable *Dictionnaire de musique* (1768).

Lettre sur la musique francaise [1]
[*1753*]

TO THE READER

Since the quarrel which arose last year at the Opéra produced nothing but abuse, bestowed by the one party with much wit and by the other with much animosity, I was unwilling to take any part in it, for that kind of contest was wholly unsuited to me and I was well aware that it was not a time to speak only reason. Now that the buffoons are dismissed, or the next thing to it, and there is no more question of cabals, I think I may venture my opinion, and I shall state it with my customary frankness, without fear of offending anyone by so doing. It even seems to me that in a subject of this kind, any reserve would be an affront to my readers, for I admit that I should have a poor opinion of a people who attached a ridiculous importance to their songs, who made more of their musicians than of their philosophers, and among whom one

1 Text: The original edition (Paris, 1753).

needed to speak more circumspectly of music than of the gravest questions of morality.

Do YOU remember, sir, the story, told by M. de Fontenelle,[2] of the Silesian infant who was born with a golden tooth? Immediately all the doctors of Germany exhausted themselves in learned disquisitions on how it was possible to be born with a golden tooth; the last thing that anyone thought of was to verify the fact; and it was found that the tooth was not golden. To avoid a similar embarrassment, it would be well, before speaking of the excellence of our music, to make sure of its existence, and to examine first, not whether it is made of gold, but whether we have one.

The Germans, the Spaniards, and the English have long claimed to possess a music peculiar to their own language; they had, in fact, national operas [3] which they admired in perfect good faith, and they were firmly persuaded that their glory would be at stake if they allowed those masterpieces, insupportable to any ears but their own, to be abolished. Pleasure has at last prevailed over vanity with them, or, at least, they have found a pleasure more easily understood in sacrificing to taste and to reason the prejudices which often make nations ridiculous by the very honor which they attach to them.

We still have in France the same feeling about our music that they had then about theirs, but who will give us the assurance that because we have been more stubborn, our obstinacy has been better grounded? Would it not then be fitting, in order to form a proper judgment of French music, that we should for once try to test it in the crucible of reason and see if it can endure the ordeal?

It is not my intention to delve deeply into this subject; that is not the business of a letter; perhaps it is not mine. I wish only to try to establish certain principles by which, until better have been found, the masters of the art, or rather the philosophers, may direct their researches; for, as a sage once said, it is the office of the poet to write poetry and that of the musician to compose music, but it is the province only of the philosopher to discuss the one and the other well.[4]

·   ·   ·   ·   ·

2 Bernard Le Bovier de Fontenelle (1657–1757), *littérateur*, perpetual secretary of the Académie des Beaux-Arts, and author of the famous remark, "Sonate, que me veux-tu?"

3 What is within limits true of Germany, and to a lesser extent of Spain, is not valid for the English scene. The period coincides with the decline of Italian opera in London and the rise of two indigenous substitutes, ballad opera and oratorio.

4 Omitted here is an extended section wherein Rousseau seeks to prove that the Italian language is best suited for musical setting.

The Italians pretend that our melody is flat and devoid of tune, and all the neutral nations [a] unanimously confirm their judgment on this point. On our side we accuse their music of being bizarre and baroque.[b] I had rather believe that both are mistaken than be reduced to saying that in countries where the sciences and the arts have arrived at so high a degree of perfection, music has still to be born.

The least partial among us [c] content themselves with saying that Italian music and French music are both good, each in its kind, each for its own language; but besides the refusal of other nations to agree to this parity, there still remains the question, which of the two languages is by its nature adapted to the best kind of music. This is a question much agitated in France, but which will never be agitated elsewhere, a question which can be decided only by an ear perfectly impartial, and which consequently becomes every day more difficult to resolve in the only country in which it is a problem. Here are some experiments on this subject which everyone is free to verify, and which, it seems to me, can serve to give the answer, at least so far as regards melody, to which alone almost the whole dispute is reducible.

I took, in the two kinds of music, airs equally esteemed, each in its own kind, and divesting them, the one of its *ports-de-voix* [5] and its perpetual cadenzas, the other of the implied notes which the composer does not trouble to write, but leaves to the discretion of the singer [d]; I sol-fa'd them exactly by note, without any ornament and without adding anything of my own to the sense or connection of the phrases. I will not tell you what effect this comparison produced upon my mind, because I have the right to offer my reasons but not to impose my authority. I merely report to you the means which I adopted to form my own opinion, in order that you, in turn, may employ them yourself if you find them good. I must warn you only that this experiment requires more precautions than one

---

a There was a time, says Milord Shaftesbury, when the practice of speaking French had made French music fashionable among us. But Italian music, by giving us a nearer view of nature, soon gave us a distaste for the other and made us see it as dull, as flat, and as doleful as it really is.

b It seems to me that people no longer dare make this reproach so frequently since it has been heard in our country. Thus this admirable music has only to show itself as it is in order to clear itself of all the faults of which it is accused.

c Many condemn the total exclusion of French music unhesitatingly pronounced by the amateurs of music; these conciliatory moderates would have no exclusive tastes, as if the love of what is good ought to compel a love of what is bad.

d This procedure gives all the advantages to the French music, for the implied notes in Ital-ian music are no less of the essence of the melody than those which are written out. It is less a question of what is written than of what should be sung, and this manner of writing notes ought simply to pass as a sort of abbreviation; whereas the cadenzas and *ports-de-voix* of French music are indeed, if you will, demanded by the style, but are not essential to the melody; they are a kind of make-up which covers its ugliness without removing it and which only makes it the more ridiculous to sensitive ears.

5 A specifically French *agrément*, an upward resolving appoggiatura executed by means of a mordent. See musical illustration in Rousseau's *Dictionnaire de musique* (Paris, 1768), Plate B, Figure 13.

would think. The first and most difficult of all is that one must maintain good faith and be equally fair in choosing and in judging. The second is that, in order to attempt this examination, one must necessarily be equally acquainted with both styles; otherwise the one which happened to be the more familiar would constantly present itself to the prejudice of the other. And this second condition is hardly easier than the first, for of all those who are well acquainted with both kinds of music, no one hesitates in his choice, and one can tell from the absurdly confused arguments of those who have undertaken to attack Italian music, how much they know of it and of the art in general.

I must add that it is essential to proceed in exact time, but I foresee that this warning, superfluous in any other country, will be quite useless in France, and this sole omission necessarily involves incompetence in judgment.

With all these precautions taken, the character of each kind of music is not slow in declaring itself, and then it is quite hard not to clothe the phrases with the ideas which are suited to them and not to add to them, at least mentally, the turns and ornaments which one is able to refuse them in singing; nor must one rest the matter on a single trial, for one air may give more pleasure than another without determining which kind of music has the preference, and a rational judgment can be formed only after a great number of trials. Besides, by foregoing a knowledge of the words, one remains ignorant of the most important element in the melody, namely the expression, and all that can be determined in this way is whether the modulation is good and whether the tune is natural and beautiful. All this shows us how hard it is to take enough precautions against prejudice and what great need we have of reasoning to put us in a condition to form a sane judgment in matters of taste.

I made another experiment which requires fewer precautions and which may perhaps seem more decisive. I gave to Italians the most beautiful airs of Lully to sing, and to French musicians some airs of Leo [6] and of Pergolesi, and I observed that while the French singers were very far from apprehending the true taste of these pieces, they were still sensible of their melody and drew from them in their own fashion melodious, agreeable, and well-cadenced musical phrases. But the Italians, while they sol-fa'd our most pathetic airs with the greatest exactness, could never recognize in them either the phrasing or the time; for them it was not a kind of music which made sense, but only a series of notes set down with-

---

6 Leonardo Leo (1694–1744), one of the opera composers of the Neapolitan school and the teacher of Jommelli, who is mentioned below.

out choice and as it were at random; they sang them precisely as you would read Arabic words written in French characters.[e]

Third experiment. I saw at Venice an Armenian, a man of intelligence, who had never heard any music, and in whose presence were performed, in the same concert, a French monologue which began with these words:

Temple sacré, séjour tranquille,[7]

and an air of Galuppi, which began with these:

Voi che languite
Senza speranza.

Both were sung, the French piece indifferently and the Italian badly, by a man familiar only with French music and at that time a great enthusiast for that of M. Rameau. I observed that during the French song the Armenian showed more surprise than pleasure, but everybody observed that from the first bars of the Italian air his face and his eyes grew soft; he was enchanted; he surrendered his soul to the impressions of the music; and though he understood little of the language, the mere sounds visibly enraptured him. From that moment he could not be induced to listen to any French air.

But without seeking examples elsewhere, have we not even among us many persons who, knowing no opera but our own, believe in good faith that they have no taste for singing and are disabused only by the Italian intermezzi? It is precisely because they like only the true music that they think they do not like music.

I allow that the great number of its faults has made me doubt the existence of our melody and has made me suspect that it might well be only a sort of modulated plainsong which has nothing agreeable in itself and which pleases only with the aid of certain arbitrary ornaments, and then only such persons as have agreed to consider them beautiful. Thus our music is hardly endurable to our own ears when it is performed by mediocre voices lacking the art to make it effective. It takes a Fel or a Jélyotte [8] to sing French music, but any voice is good in Italian music, because the beauties of Italian singing are in the music itself, whereas

---

[e] Our musicians profess to derive a great advantage from this difference. "We can perform Italian music," they say, with their customary pride, "and the Italians cannot perform ours; therefore our music is better than theirs." They fail to see that they ought to draw a quite contrary conclusion and say, "therefore the Italians have melody and we have none."

[7] From Rameau's *Hippolyte et Aricie* (text by Simon Joseph Pelegrin) performed in 1733: Act I, Scene I (*Oeuvres complètes*, VI, 53).

[8] Marie Fel (1713–1794) and Pierre Jélyotte (1713–1797), the two leading singers of the French lyric stage, are best known for their performances in traditional French opera. Although they sang in Rousseau's *Le Devin du village*, they avoided taking sides in the aesthetic battle of the time.

those of French singing, if there are any, are all in the art of the singer.[f]

Three things seem to me to unite in contributing to the perfection of Italian melody. The first is the softness of the language, which makes all the inflections easy and leaves the taste of the musician free to make a more exquisite choice among them, to give a greater variety to his combinations, and to provide each singer with a particular style of singing, so that each man has the character and tone which are proper to him and distinguish him from other men.

The second is the boldness of the modulations, which, although less servilely prepared than our own, are much more pleasing from being made more perceptible, and without imparting any harshness to the song, add a lively energy to the expression. It is by this means that the musician, passing abruptly from one key or mode to another, and suppressing, when necessary, the intermediate and pedantic transitions, is able to express the reticences, the interruptions, the falterings, which are the language of impetuous passion so often employed by the ardent Metastasio, which a Porpora, a Galuppi, a Cocchi, a Jommelli, a Perez, a Terradellas have so often successfully reproduced,[9] and of which our lyric poets know as little as do our musicians.

The third advantage, the one which gives to melody its greatest effect, is the extreme exactness of time which is felt in the slowest as well as in the liveliest movements, an exactness which makes the singing animated and interesting, the accompaniments lively and rhythmical; which really multiplies the tunes by making as many different melodies out of a single combination of sounds as there are ways of scanning them; which conveys every sentiment to the heart and every picture to the mind; which enables the musician to express in his air all the imaginable characters of words, many of which we have no idea of; [g] and which renders all the movements

---

[f] Besides, it is a mistake to believe that the Italian singers generally have less voice than the French. On the contrary they must have a stronger and more harmonious resonance to make themselves heard in the immense theaters of Italy without ceasing to keep the sound under the control which Italian music requires. French singing demands all the power of the lungs, the whole extent of the voice. "Louder," say our singing masters; "more volume; open your mouth; use all your voice." "Softer," say the Italian masters; "don't force it; sing at your ease; make your notes soft, flexible, and flowing; save the outbursts for those rare, brief moments when you must astonish and overwhelm." Now it seems to me that when it is necessary to make oneself heard, the man who can do so without screaming must have the stronger voice.

[g] Not to depart from the comic style, the only one known to Paris, consider the airs, "Quando sciolto avrò il contratto," "Io ho un vespaio," "O questo o quello t'hai a risolvere," "Ha un gusto da stordire," "Stizzoso mio, stizzoso," "Io sono una donzella," "Quanti maestri, quanti dottori," "I sbirri già lo aspettano," "Ma dunque il testamento," "Senti me, se brami stare, o che risa! che piacere!" all characters of airs of which French music has not the first elements and of which it is incapable of expressing a single word.

[9] Niccolò Antonio Porpora (1686–1766), Baldassare Galuppi, often called Buranello after his birthplace (1706–1785), Gioacchino Cocchi (1715–1804), Niccolò Jommelli (1714–1774), Davide Perez (1711–1778), Domenico Terradellas (1711–1751); with the exception of the *buffa* composer Galuppi, largely a list of the more prominent opera composers associated with the Neapolitan school. Galuppi was performed by the Italian

proper to express all the characters,[h] or at the will of the composer renders a single movement proper to contrast and change the character.

These, in my opinion, are the sources from which Italian music derives its charms and its energy, to which may be added a new and strong proof of the advantage of its melody, in that it does not require so often as ours those frequent inversions of harmony which give to the thorough bass a melody worthy of a soprano. Those who find such great beauties in French melody might very well tell us to which of these things it owes them or show us the advantages it has to take their place.

On first acquaintance with Italian melody, one finds in it only graces and believes it suited only to express agreeable sentiments, but with the least study of its pathetic and tragic character, one is soon surprised by the force imparted to it by the art of the composer in their great pieces of music. It is by the aid of these scientific modulations, of this simple and pure harmony, of these lively and brilliant accompaniments that their divine performances harrow or enrapture the soul, carry away the spectator, and force from him, in his transports, the cries with which our placid operas were never honored.

How does the musician succeed in producing these grand effects? Is it by contrasting the movements, by multiplying the harmonies, the notes, the parts? Is it by heaping design upon design, instrument upon instrument? Any such jumble, which is only a bad substitute where genius is lacking, would stifle the music instead of enlivening it and would destroy the interest by dividing the attention. Whatever harmony several parts, each perfectly melodious, may be capable of producing together, the effect of these beautiful melodies disappears as soon as they are heard simultaneously, and there is heard only a chord succession, which one may say is always lifeless when not animated by melody; so that the more one heaps up inappropriate melodies, the less the music is pleasing and melodious, because it is impossible for the ear to follow several melodies at once, and as one effaces the impression of another, the sum total is only noise and confusion. For a piece of music to become interesting, for it to convey to the soul the sentiments which it is intended to arouse, all the parts must concur in reinforcing the impression of the subject: the harmony must serve only to make it more energetic; the accompaniment

---

troupe, but few of the works of the others appeared on the Paris stage, their operas gaining standing by performances of isolated arias and by the accounts of those who had heard them elsewhere.

[h] I shall content myself with citing a single

example, but a very striking one: the air, "Se pur d'un infelice," in *The Intriguing Chambermaid* [*La Finta cameriera*], a very pathetic air with a very lively movement, which lacks only a voice to sing it, an orchestra to accompany it, ears to hear it, and the second part, which should not be suppressed.

must embellish it without covering it up or disfiguring it; the bass, by a uniform and simple progression, must somehow guide the singer and the listener without either's perceiving it; in a word, the entire ensemble must at one time convey only one melody to the ear and only one idea to the mind.

This unity of melody seems to me to be an indispensable rule, no less important in music than the unity of action in tragedy, for it is based on the same principle and directed toward the same object. Thus all the good Italian composers conform to it with a care which sometimes degenerates into affectation, and with the least reflection one soon perceives that from it their music derives its principal effect. It is in this great rule that one must seek the cause of the frequent accompaniments in unison which are observed in Italian music and which, reinforcing the idea of the melody, at the same time render its notes more soft and mellow and less tiring for the voice. These unisons are not practicable in our music, unless it be in some types of airs chosen for the purpose and adapted to it. A pathetic French air would never be tolerable if accompanied in this manner, because, as vocal and instrumental music with us have different characters, we cannot employ in the one the same devices which suit the other without offending against the melody and the style; leaving out of account that as the time is always vague and undetermined, especially in slow airs, the instruments and the voice would never be in agreement and would not keep step well enough to produce a pleasing effect together. A further beauty resulting from these unisons is to give a more sensible expression to the vocal melody, now by letting it unexpectedly reinforce the instruments in a passage, now by letting it make them more tender, now by letting it give them some striking, energetic phrase of the melody of which it is itself incapable, but for which the listener, skillfully deceived, never fails to give it credit when the orchestra knows how to bring it to the fore at the right moment. From this arises also that perfect correspondence between the ritornelli and the melody, as the result of which all the strokes which we admire in the one are only the development of the other, so that the source of all the beauties of the accompaniment is always to be sought in the vocal part; this accompaniment is so wholly of a piece with the singing and corresponds so exactly to the words that it often seems to determine the action and to dictate to the actor the gesture which he is to make,[1] and an actor who would be incapable of playing the part with

---

[1] Numerous examples may be found in the intermezzi which have been performed for us this year, among others in the air "Ha un gusto di stordire" in *The Music Master* [*Il Maestro di musica*]; in that of "Son padrone" in *The Vain Woman* [*La Donna superba*]; in that of "Vi stò ben" in *Tracollo;* in that of "Tu non pensi" in *The Bohemian* [*La Zingara*]; and in nearly all of those which require acting.

the words alone might play it very correctly with the music, because the music performs so well its function of interpreter.

Besides this, the Italian accompaniments are very far from always being in unison with the voice. There are two very frequent cases in which the music separates them. One is when the voice, lightly singing a passage over a series of harmonies, so holds the attention that the accompaniment cannot share it; yet even then this accompaniment is made so simple that the ear, affected only by agreeable harmonies, does not perceive in them any harmony which could distract it.

The other case demands a little more effort to be comprehended. "When the musician understands his art," says the author of the *Letter on the Deaf and Dumb*,[10] "the parts of the accompaniment concur either in reinforcing the expression of the vocal part, or in adding new ideas demanded by the subject and beyond the capacity of the vocal part to express." This passage seems to me to contain a very useful precept, and this is how I think it should be understood.

If the vocal part is of such a nature as to require some additions, or as our old musicians used to say, some divisions, which add to the expression or to the agreeableness without thereby destroying the unity of the melody, so that the ear, which would perhaps blame them if made by the voice, approves of them in the accompaniment and allows itself to be gently affected without being made less attentive to the vocal part, then the skillful musician, by managing them properly and disposing them with taste, will embellish his subject and give it more expression without impairing its unity; and although the accompaniment will not be exactly like the vocal part, the two will nevertheless constitute only a single air and a single melody. For if the sense of the words connotes some accessory idea, the musician will superimpose this during the pauses of the voice or while it sustains some note, and will thus be able to present it to the hearer without distracting him from the idea expressed by the voice. The advantage will be still greater if this accessory idea can be expressed by a restrained and continuous accompaniment, producing a slight murmur rather than a real melody, like the sound of a river or the twittering of birds, for then the composer can completely separate the vocal part from the accompaniment, and assigning to the latter only the expression of the accessory idea, he will dispose his vocal part in such a way as to give frequent openings to the orchestra, taking care to insure that the instrumental part is always dominated by the vocal, a matter depending more upon the art of the composer than on the execution of the instruments;

---

10 One of the many anonymous pamphlets supporting Italian music.

but this demands a consummate experience, in order to avoid a double melody.

This is all that the rule of unity can concede to the taste of the musician in order to ornament the singing or to make it more expressive, whether by embellishing the principal subject or by adding to this another which remains subordinate. But to make the violins play by themselves on one side, the flutes on another, the bassoons on a third, each with a special motive and almost without any mutual relation, and to call all this chaos music is to insult alike the ear and the judgment of the hearers.

. . . . .

I hope, sir, that you will pardon me the length of this article, out of consideration for the novelty and the importance of its aim. I have felt it my duty to enlarge somewhat upon so essential a rule as that of the unity of melody, a rule of which no theorist, to my knowledge, has to this day spoken, which the Italian composers alone have felt and practiced, perhaps without suspecting its existence, a rule on which depend the sweetness of the melody, the force of the expression, and almost all the charm of good music. Before I leave this subject, it remains for me to show you that from it result new advantages for harmony itself, at the expense of which I seemed to be bestowing all the advantages upon melody, and that the expression of the melody gives occasion to that of the harmony by forcing the composer to dispose them with art.

Do you recall, sir, having sometimes heard the son of the Italian impresario, a boy of ten years at the most, accompany the intermezzi which were given here at the Opéra this year? We were struck, from the first day, by the effect produced by his little fingers in the accompaniment on the harpsichord, and the whole audience perceived, from his exact and brilliant playing, that he was not the usual accompanist. I at once sought for the reasons of this difference, for I had no doubt that the Sieur Noblet [11] was a good harmonist and accompanied very exactly, but what was my surprise, as I watched the hands of the little fellow, to see that he almost never filled out the chords, and that he suppressed many notes, very often using only two fingers, one of which nearly always sounded the octave of the bass. "What!" said I to myself, "the complete harmony has less effect than the harmony mutilated, and our accompanists, filling out all the chords, produce only a confused sound, while this one, with fewer notes, creates more harmony, or at least makes his harmony

11 Charles Noblet, accompanist at the Opéra until 1762. He composed sacred music heard at the Concerts Spirituels and published two "livres de clavecin" (1754, 1756).

more distinct and more pleasing!" The problem perplexed me. I understood its importance even better, when upon further observation I saw that all the Italians accompanied in the same manner as the little boy, and that consequently this economy in their accompaniment must depend on the same principle as that which they follow in their score.

I well understood how the bass, being the foundation of all harmony, should always prevail over the rest, and that when the other parts stifle it or cover it up, this causes a confusion which makes the harmony less distinct; and I saw in this the reason why the Italians, so economical with the right hand in accompanying, ordinarily play the octave of the bass with the left; why they have so many double basses in their orchestras; and why they so often make their violas [j] proceed with the bass, instead of giving them a separate part as the French never fail to do. But this, which accounted for the precision of the harmonies, did not account for their energy, and I soon saw that there must be some subtler and less obvious principle in the expressiveness which I observed in the simplicity of Italian harmony while I found our own so complicated, cold, and languid.

I remembered then to have read in some work of M. Rameau that each consonance has its particular character, that is to say, a manner peculiar to itself of affecting the soul; that the effect of the third is not at all the same as that of the fifth, nor that of the fourth the same as that of the sixth; similarly the minor thirds and sixths must affect us differently from the major. Granting this, it follows clearly enough that the dissonances and all the intervals possible will be in the same case. This experience is confirmed by reason, since whenever the relations are different the impressions cannot be the same.

Now in reasoning from this hypothesis I reflected: "I see clearly that two consonances added together inappropriately, although according to the rules of harmony, may, even while increasing the harmony, weaken, oppose, or divide each other's effect. If the whole effect of a fifth is required for the expression which I need, I may well risk weakening that expression if I introduce a third sound which, interposing two other intervals within this fifth, will necessarily modify its effect by adding that of the two thirds into which I have resolved it; and even if the whole combination makes a very good harmony, these thirds themselves, being of different species, may still reciprocally impair each other's effect. In

---

[j] One can observe in the orchestra of our Opéra that in Italian music the violas almost never play their part when it doubles the bass at the octave: perhaps in these circumstances they do not deign to copy the bass. Are the conductors of the orchestra unaware that the lack of connection between the bass and the treble makes the harmony too dry?

like manner, if I needed the simultaneous impression of the fifth and the two thirds, I should weaken that impression and change it for the worse if I suppressed one of the three notes forming the consonance.

"This argument becomes even more apparent when applied to dissonance. Suppose that I have need of all the harshness of the tritone or all the colorlessness of the diminished fifth (a contrast, by the way, which shows how much the effect of an interval can be changed by inversion); if, in such circumstances, instead of conveying to the ear only two sounds which form the dissonance, I am minded to complete the chord with all the notes belonging to it, then I add to the tritone the second and the sixth and to the diminished fifth the sixth and the third; that is, by introducing into each of these chords a new dissonance, I introduce at the same time three consonances which must necessarily temper and weaken its effect by making one of these consonances more colorful and the other less harsh."

It is therefore a certain principle, and one based on nature, that all music in which the harmony is scrupulously filled out, every accompaniment in which all the harmonies are complete, must make a great deal of noise but have very little expression. This is precisely the character of French music. It is true that in regulating the harmonies and the part-leading, the selection becomes difficult and demands much experience and taste if it is always to be made suitably; but if there is one rule to help the composer acquit himself well on such occasion, it is surely that of the unity of melody which I have tried to establish, and which is in conformity with the character of Italian music and accounts for the sweetness of the melody together with the force of expression which prevails in it.

From all this it follows that after a thorough study of the elementary rules of harmony, the musician must not hasten to be inconsiderately lavish of it, nor believe himself ready to compose because he knows how to fill out the harmonies; but that before setting hand to the much longer and more difficult study of the various impressions which the consonances, the dissonances, and all the harmonies make on sensitive ears, he must often remind himself that the great art of the composer consists no less in knowing on occasion which notes to leave out than in knowing which to use. It is by studying and continually turning the pages of the master-pieces of Italy that he will learn how to make that delicate choice, if nature has given him enough genius and taste to feel its necessity. For the difficulties of the art are visible only to those who are born to overcome them, and such men will not be of a mind to look with disdain on the vacant spaces in a score, but seeing the ease with which a pupil could have filled them, they will suspect and look for the reasons for this deceptive simplicity, the more admirable because beneath a feigned negligence it conceals prodigies, and because *l'arte che tutto fa, nulla si scuopre* ("the art which does all remains invisible").

Here, in my opinion, is the cause of the surprising effects produced by the harmony of Italian music, although much less burdened than that of our own, which produces so few. This does not mean that the harmony must never be full, but that it must be made full only with selection and discernment. Neither is it to say that to make this selection the musician is obliged to go through this reasoning, but that he should be sensible of its result. It is for him to have the taste and the genius to discover the things that are effective; it is for the theorist to investigate the causes and to say why these things are effective.

If you cast your eye on our modern compositions and especially if you hear them played, you will soon recognize that our musicians have so little understood all this that in striving to arrive at the same goal they have followed the directly opposite road, and if I may be allowed to state my frank opinion, I find that the further our music advances toward apparent perfection, the more it is actually deteriorating.

It was perhaps necessary that it should reach its present state, in order that our ears might insensibly become accustomed to reject the prejudices of habit and to enjoy other airs than those with which our nurses sang us to sleep; but I foresee that to bring it to the very mediocre degree of merit of which it is capable, we shall sooner or later have to begin by once more descending (or reascending) to the state to which Lully brought it. Let us agree that the harmony of that famous musician is purer and less inverted; that his basses are more natural and proceed more directly; that his melody is more flowing; that his accompaniments, less burdened, spring more truly from the subject and depart from it less; that his recitative is much less mannered than ours, and consequently much better. This is confirmed by the style of the execution, for the old recitative was sung by the actors of that time in a way wholly different from that of today. It was livelier and less dragging; it was sung less and declaimed more.[k] In our recitative the cadenzas and *ports-de-voix* have been multiplied; it has become still more languid and has hardly anything left to distinguish it from what we call "air."

Now that airs and recitatives have been mentioned, you will permit me, sir, to conclude this letter with some observations on the one and the

---

[k] This is proved by the time of the representation of Lully's operas, much longer now than in his day by the unanimous report of those who have seen them long ago. Thus, whenever these operas are revived, they call for considerable cutting.

other which will perhaps throw some helpful light on the solution of the problem involved.

One may judge of the idea our musicians have of the nature of an opera by the singularity of their nomenclature. Those grand pieces of Italian music which ravish the soul, those masterpieces of genius which draw tears, which offer the most striking pictures, which paint the liveliest situations and fill the soul with all the passions they express, the French call "ariettes." They give the name of "airs" to those insipid little ditties which they interpolate in the scenes of their operas, and reserve that of "monologues" particularly to those long-drawn-out and tedious lamentations which if only sung in tune and without screams would put everybody to sleep.

In the Italian opera all the airs grow out of the situation and form a part of the scene. Now a despairing father imagines he sees the ghost of a son whom he has unjustly put to death upbraid him with his cruelty; now an easygoing prince, compelled to give an example of severity, entreats the gods to deprive him of his rule or to give him a less susceptible heart. Here a tender mother weeps to recover her son whom she thought dead; there we hear the language of love, not filled with that insipid rigmarole of "flames" and "chains," [12] but tragic, animated, ardent, and faltering, and befitting impetuous passion. Upon such words it is appropriate to lavish all the wealth of a music full of force and expression and to enhance the energy of the poetry by that of harmony and melody.

The words of our ariettes, on the contrary, always detached from the subject, are only a wretched medley of honeyed phrases which one is only too glad not to understand. They are a random assemblage of the small number of sonorous words that our language can furnish, turned and twisted in every manner except the one that might give them some meaning. It is upon such impertinent nonsense that our musicians exhaust their taste and knowledge and our actors waste their gestures and lungs; it is over these extravagant pieces that our women go into ecstasies of admiration. And the most striking proof that French music is incapable of either description or expression is that it cannot display the few beauties at its command except upon words which have no meaning.

Meanwhile, to hear the French talk of music, one would imagine that in their operas it depicts great scenes and great passions, and that only ariettes are found in Italian operas, to which the very word "ariette" and the ridiculous thing it signifies are equally unknown. We must not be sur-

---

12 The special attention given to the musical setting of such words in the *tragédie-lyrique* grew out of classical French declamation. Cf. Grétry, who has the same complaint (p. 141 below); or Diderot, in his *Neveu de Rameau* (*Oeuvres complètes*, V, 461 f.).

prised by the grossness of these prejudices: Italian music has no enemies, even among ourselves, but those who know nothing about it, and all Frenchmen who have tried to study it with the sole aim of criticizing it understandingly have soon become its most zealous admirers.[1]

After the "ariettes," which constitute the triumph of modern taste in Paris, come the famous monologues which are admired in our old operas. In this connection it is to be noted that our most beautiful airs are always in the monologues and never in the scenes, for, as our actors have no art of pantomime and the music does not indicate any gesture or depict any situation, the one who remains silent has no notion what to do with himself while the other is singing.

The drawling nature of our language, the little flexibility of our voices, and the doleful tone which perpetually reigns in our opera, give a slow tempo to nearly all our French monologues, and as the time or beat is not made perceptible either in the melody or in the bass or in the accompaniment, nothing drags so much or is so relaxed, so languid, as these beautiful monologues, which everybody admires while he yawns; they aim to be sad and are only tiresome; they aim to touch the heart and only distress the ear.

The Italians are more adroit in their Adagios, for when the time is so slow that there is any danger of weakening the sense of the rhythm, they make their bass proceed by notes of equal value which mark the movement, while the accompaniment also marks it by subdivisions of the beats, which, keeping the voice and the ear in time, make the melody more pleasing and above all more energetic by this exactness. But the nature of French music forbids our composers this resource, for if the actor were compelled to keep time, he would immediately be prevented from displaying his voice and his action, from dwelling on his notes, from swelling and prolonging them, and from screaming at the top of his lungs, and in consequence he would no longer be applauded.

But what still more effectively prevents monotony and boredom in the Italian tragedies is the advantage of being able to express all the passions and depict all the characters in whatever measure and time the composer pleases. Our melody, which in itself expresses nothing, derives all its expression from the tempo one gives to it. It is of necessity sad in a slow tempo, furious or gay in a lively one, serious in a moderate one; the melody itself counts for almost nothing in this; the tempo alone, or, to put it more accurately, the degree of rapidity alone determines the

---

[1] A presupposition little favorable to French music appears in this: those who despise it most are precisely those who know it best, for it is as ridiculous when examined as it is intolerable when heard.

character. But Italian melody finds in every tempo expressions for all characters, pictures for all objects. When the musician so chooses, it is sad in a slow tempo, and, as I have already said, it changes character in the same movement at the pleasure of the composer. Contrasts are thereby made easy, without depending for this on the poet and without the risk of conflicts with the sense.

Here is the source of that prodigious variety which the great masters of Italy were able to display in their operas without ever departing from nature, a variety which prevents monotony, languor, and ennui, and which French musicians cannot imitate because their tempi are prescribed by the sense of the words and they are forced to adhere to them unless they are willing to fall into ridiculous inconsistencies.

With regard to the recitative, of which it remains for me to speak, it seems to me that to judge it properly we must begin by knowing exactly what it is, for of all those who have discussed it I am so far unaware of any one who has thought of defining it. I do not know, sir, what idea you may have of that word; as for myself, I call recitative a harmonious declamation, that is, a declamation of which all the inflections are formed by harmonious intervals. It therefore follows that as each language has its own peculiar declamation, each language ought also to have its own peculiar recitative. This does not preclude one from very properly comparing one recitative with another to discover which of the two is the better, that is, the better adapted to its purpose.

Recitative is necessary in lyric drama, first, to connect the action and preserve the unity; second, to set off the airs, of which a continuous succession would be insupportable; third, to express a number of things which cannot be expressed by lyric, cadenced music. Mere declamation cannot be suitable for all that in a lyric work, because the transition from speech to song and especially that from song to speech has an abruptness which the ear does not readily accept, and presents a shocking contrast which destroys all the illusion and in consequence the interest.[13] For there is a kind of probability which must be preserved even at the Opéra, by making the language so homogeneous that the whole may at least be taken for a hypothetical language. Add to this that the aid of the harmonies augments the energy of musical declamation and compensates advantageously for what is less natural in its intonations.

It is evident, according to these notions, that the best recitative, in any language whatever, if this language fulfills the necessary conditions, is

---

13 Rousseau refers to the Opéra Comique, which was then giving performances of mixed song and declamation (*comédies mêlées d'ariettes*) at the fairs of St. Germain and St. Laurent.

that which comes the nearest to speaking; if there were one which came so near to it as to deceive the ear or the mind while still preserving the required harmony, one might boldly pronounce that it had attained to the highest perfection of which any recitative is capable.

Let us now examine by this rule what in France is called "recitative." I pray you, tell me what relation you find between that recitative and our declamation. How can you ever conceive that the French language, of which the accent is so uniform, so simple, so modest, so unlike that of song, can be properly rendered by the shrill and noisy intonations of that recitative, and that there should be any relation whatever between the soft inflection of speech and these prolonged and exaggerated sounds, or rather these perpetual shrieks which form the tissue of that part of our music even more than that of the airs? For instance, let anyone who knows how to read recite the first four lines of the famous recognition scene of Iphigénie; you will barely detect a few slight inequalities, a few feeble inflections of the voice, in a tranquil recital which has nothing lively or impassioned, nothing which compels the speaker to raise or lower the voice. Then have one of our actresses deliver the same lines as set to music by the composer, and try, if you can, to endure that extravagant shrieking which shifts at each moment from low to high and from high to low, traverses without a subject the whole vocal register, and interrupts the recital in the wrong place to string some beautiful notes upon syllables without meaning, which correspond to no pause in the sense. Add to this the *fredons*,[14] cadenzas, and *ports-de-voix* which recur at every moment, and tell me what analogy there can be between speech and this pretended recitative, or at least show me some ground on which one may find reason to vaunt this wonderful French recitative whose invention is Lully's title to glory.

It is very amusing to see the partisans of French music take refuge in the character of the language and attribute to it the faults of which they do not dare to accuse their idol, whereas it is evident on all grounds that the recitative most suitable to the French language must be almost the opposite of that which is in use; that it must range within very small intervals, without much raising or lowering of the voice; with few prolonged notes, no sudden outbursts, still fewer shrieks; especially, nothing which resembles melody; little inequality in the duration or value of the notes or in their intensity either. In a word, the true French recitative, if one is possible, will be found only by a path directly opposite to that taken by Lully and his successors, by some new path which assuredly the French

---

14 Literally a short roulade, here implying excessive ornamentation.

composers, so proud of their false learning and consequently so far from feeling and loving what is true, will not soon be willing to seek and which they will probably never find.

Here would be the place to show you, by the example of Italian recitative, that all the conditions which I have postulated in a good recitative can actually be found there; that it can have at the same time all the vivacity and all the energy of harmony; that it can proceed as rapidly as speech and be as melodious as veritable song; that it can indicate all the inflections with which the most vehement passions animate discourse, without straining the voice of the singer or deafening the ears of the listeners. I could show you how, with the aid of a particular basic progression, one may multiply the modulations of the recitative in a way suitable to it and which contributes to distinguishing it from the airs when, in order to preserve the graces of the melody, the key must be less frequently changed; how, especially, when one wishes to give passion the time to display all its movements, it is possible, by means of a skillfully managed interlude, to make the orchestra express by varied and pathetic phrases what the actor can only relate—a master stroke of the musician's art, by which, in an accompanied recitative,[m] he may combine the most affecting melody with all the vehemence of declamation without ever confusing the one with the other. I could unfold to you all the numberless beauties of that admirable recitative of which in France so many absurd tales are told, as absurd as the judgments which people presume to pass on them, as if one could judge of a recitative without a thorough knowledge of the language to which it belongs. But to enter into these details it would be necessary, so to speak, to create a new dictionary, to coin terms every moment in order to present to French readers ideas unknown among them, and to address them in language which would seem meaningless to them. In a word, one would be obliged, in order to make oneself clear, to speak a language they understood, and consequently to speak of any science or art whatever except music alone. Therefore I shall not go into this subject with an affected detail which would do nothing to instruct my readers and concerning which they might presume that I owed the apparent force of my arguments only to their ignorance in this matter.

For the same reason I shall also not attempt what was proposed this

m I had hoped that Signor Caffarelli would give us, in the concert of sacred music, some example of grand recitative and of pathetic melody, in order to let the pretended connoisseurs hear for once what they have so long been passing judgment on, but I found, from his reasons for doing nothing of the kind, that he knew better than I the capacity of his hearers.

[Gaetano Majorano, called Caffarelli after his earliest protector (1703–1783), one of the leading Italian castrati. Louis XV engaged him to entertain the Dauphine, according to the *Mémoires du duc de Luynes* (XII, 471 and XIII, 10), and while in Paris he was also heard at the Concert Spirituel on November 5, 1753—an event which Rousseau presumably attended.—Ed.]

winter in a publication addressed to the "Little Prophet" and his opponents, a comparison between two pieces of music, the one Italian and
the other French, which were there indicated.

.   .   .   .   .

I think that I have shown that there is neither measure nor melody in
French music, because the language is not capable of them; that French
singing is a continual squalling, insupportable to an unprejudiced ear;
that its harmony is crude and devoid of expression and suggests only the
padding of a pupil; that French "airs" are not airs; that French recitative
is not recitative. From this I conclude that the French have no music and
cannot have any; [n] or that if they ever have, it will be so much the worse
for them.[15]

I am, etc.

---

[n] I do not call it having a music to import that
of another language and try to apply it to one's
own, and I had rather we kept our wretched and
absurd singing than that we should still more
absurdly unite Italian melody with the French
language. This distasteful combination, which
will perhaps from now on constitute the study
of our musicians, is too monstrous to be accepted,
and the character of our language will never lend
itself to it. At most, some comic pieces will succeed in passing by reason of their orchestral part,
but I boldly predict that the tragic style will never
be attempted. At the Opéra Comique this winter
the public applauded the work of a man of talent
who seems to have listened with good ears, and
who has translated the style into French as closely
as is possible; his accompaniments are well imitated without being copied; and if he has written
no melody, it is because it is impossible to write

any. Young musicians who feel that you have
talent, continue in public to despise Italian music; I am well aware that your present interest
requires it; but in private make haste to study
that language and that music if you wish to be
able some day to turn against your comrades the
disdain which today you affect for your masters.

[15] Rousseau's blanket condemnation of French
music represents a sudden about-face. Only a few
years before, in 1750 to be exact, he had sent
Baron Grimm a comparison of French and Italian
opera. In 1750 he had found many reasons for
thinking French opera superior to Italian. Had
the letter been generally available at the time, it
would have been most embarrassing to its author.
The document is reprinted in the appendix of
Albert Jansen's *Jean-Jacques Rousseau als Mu-
siker* (Berlin, 1884), pp. 455–463.

III

Critical Views of Italian Opera:
Algarotti and Gluck

6. Francesco Algarotti

Algarotti was a man of many-sided and cosmopolitan culture. Born at Venice in 1712, he went in 1740 to Berlin on the invitation of Frederick the Great, and remained there for nine years in close touch with the King, assisting him in the translation of opera librettos. He returned to Italy in 1753 and died at Pisa in 1764.

The outstanding characteristic of Algarotti's writings is a kind of cosmopolitan dilettantism. His *Saggio sopra l'opera in musica* (1755) is of interest as the work of a highly cultured Italian, voicing critical views on contemporary Italian opera. Among his other writings, his *Lettere sulla pittura* command attention as a source of information and judicious criticism.

From *the* Saggio sopra l'opera in musica [1]
[*1755*]

I. OF THE POEM, ARGUMENT, OR BUSINESS OF AN OPERA

As soon as the desired regulation shall have been introduced on the theatre it will then be incumbent to proceed to the various constituent parts of an opera in order that those amendments should be made in each whereof they severally now appear the most deficient. The leading object to be maturely considered is the nature of the subject to be chosen, an article of much more consequence than is commonly imagined; for the success or failure of the drama depends, in a great measure, on a good or bad choice of the subject. It is here of no less consequence than, in architecture, the plan is to an edifice, or the canvas, in painting, is to a picture; because thereon the poet draws the outlines of his intended representation, and its coloring is the task of the musical composer. It is therefore the poet's duty, as chief engineer of the undertaking, to give directions to the

---

1 Text: The original edition of the anonymous English translation of 1768, pp. 14–52.

dancers, the machinists, the painters; nay, down even to those who are entrusted with the care of the wardrobe and dressing the performers. The poet is to carry in his mind a comprehensive view of the *whole* of the drama; because those parts which are not the productions of his pen ought to flow from the dictates of his actuating judgment, which is to give being and movement to the whole.

At the first institution of operas, the poets imagined the heathen mythology to be the best source from which they could derive subjects for their dramas. Hence Daphne, Eurydice, Ariadne, were made choice of by Ottavio Rinuccini and are looked upon as the eldest musical dramas, having been exhibited about the beginning of the last century. There was, besides, Poliziano's *Orpheus*,[2] which also had been represented with instrumental accompaniments, as well as another performance that was no more than a medley of dancing and music, contrived by Bergonzo Botta for the entertainment of a Duke of Milan in the city of Tortona.[3] A particular species of drama was exhibited at Venice for the amusement of Henry the Third; it had been set to music by the famous Zarlino.[4] Add to these some other performances, which ought only to be considered as so many rough sketches and preludes to a complete opera.

The intent of our poets was to revive the Greek tragedy in all its lustre and to introduce Melpomene on our stage, attended by music, dancing, and all that imperial pomp with which, at the brilliant period of a Sophocles and Euripides, she was wont to be escorted. And that such splendid pageantry might appear to be the genuine right of tragedy, the poets had recourse for their subjects to the heroic ages and heathen mythology. From that fountain, the bard, according to his inventive pleasure, introduced on the theatre all the deities of paganism; now shifting his scene to Olympus, now fixing it in the Elysian shades, now plunging it down to Tartarus, with as much ease as if to Argos or to Thebes. And thus, by the intervention of superior beings, he gave an air of probability to most surprising and wonderful events. Every circumstance being thus elevated above the sphere of mortal existence, it necessarily followed that the singing of actors in an opera appeared a true imitation of the language made use of by the deities they represented.

This then was the original cause why, in the first dramas that had been exhibited in the courts of sovereigns or the palaces of princes in order to

---

2 Performed at Mantua in 1472, or perhaps 1471; cf. Alfred Einstein, *The Italian Madrigal* (Princeton, 1949), I, 34–35.

3 The medley referred to was a festal play with music to celebrate the wedding of Gian Galeazzo Sforza and Isabella of Aragon. The performance of this unnamed work took place in 1488.

4 A reference to Cornelio Frangipane's *Proteo* of 1574, the music not by Zarlino but by Claudio Merulo; cf. Angelo Solerti, "Le rappresentazioni musicali di Venezia dal 1571 al 1605," *Rivista musicale italiana*, IX (1902), 503–558.

celebrate their nuptials, such expensive machinery was employed; not an article was omitted that could excite an idea of what is most wonderful to be seen either on earth or in the heavens. To superadd a greater diversity and thereby give a new animation to the whole, crowded choruses of singers were admitted, as well as dances of various contrivance, with a special attention that the execution of the ballet should coincide and be combined with the choral song; all which pleasing effects were made to spring naturally from the subject of the drama.

No doubt then can remain of the exquisite delight that such magic representations must have given to an enraptured assembly; for although it consisted but of a single subject, it nevertheless displayed an almost infinite variety of entertainment. There is even now frequent opportunity of seeing, on the French musical theatre, a spirited likeness to what is here advanced; because the opera was first introduced in Paris by Cardinal Mazarin, whither it carried the same magnificent apparatus with which it had made its appearance at his time in Italy.[5]

These representations must, however, have afterwards suffered not a little by the intermixture of buffoon characters, which are such ill-suited companions of the dignity of heroes and of gods; for by making the spectators laugh out of season, they disconcert the solemnity of the piece. Some traces of this theatric impropriety are even now observable in the eldest of the French musical dramas.[6]

The opera did not long remain confined in the courts of sovereigns and palaces of princes, but, emancipating itself from such thralldom, displayed its charms on public theatres, to which the curious of all ranks were admitted for pay. But in this situation, as must obviously occur to whoever reflects, it was impossible that the pomp and splendor which was attendant on this entertainment from its origin could be continued. The falling off, in that article, was occasioned principally by the exorbitant salaries the singers insisted on, which had been but inconsiderable at the first outset of the musical drama; as for instance, a certain female singer was called *La Centoventi*, "The Hundred-and-Twenty," [7] for having received so many crowns for her performance during a single carnival, a sum which hath been amazingly exceeded since, almost beyond all bounds.

Hence arose the necessity for opera directors to change their measures and to be as frugally economical on the one hand as they found themselves unavoidably profuse on the other. Through such saving, the opera may

---

5 For a list of the Italian operas performed in France between 1645 and 1662 see Alfred Loewenberg, *Annals of Opera* (Cambridge, 1943), p. 21.
6 Comic characters appear in the first three operas of Lully (*Cadmus*, 1673; *Alceste*, 1674; *Thésée*, 1675) but not in the later works.
7 This singer has not been further identified.

be said to have fallen from heaven upon the earth and, being divorced from an intercourse with gods, to have humbly resigned itself to that of mortals.

Thenceforward prevailed a general renunciation of all subjects to be found in the fabulous accounts of the heathen deities, and none were made choice of but those derived from the histories of humble mankind, because less magnificent in their nature, and therefore less liable to large disbursements for their exhibition.

The directors, obliged to circumspection for their own safety, were induced to imagine they might supply the place of all that costly pomp and splendid variety of decoration, to which the dazzled spectators had been accustomed so long, by introducing a chaster regularity into their drama, seconded by the auxiliary charms of a more poetical diction as well as by the concurring powers of a more exquisite musical composition. This project gained ground the faster from the public's observing that one of these arts was entirely employed in modeling itself on our ancient authors, and the other solely intent on enriching itself with new ornaments; which made operas to be looked upon by many as having nearly reached the pinnacle of perfection. However, that these representations might not appear too naked and uniform, interludes and ballets, to amuse the audience, were introduced between the acts; and thus, by degrees, the opera took that form which is now practised on our theatres.

It is an incontrovertible fact that subjects for an operatical drama, whether taken from pagan mythology or historians, have inevitable inconveniences annexed to them. The fabulous subjects, on account of the great number of machines and magnificent apparatus which they require, often distress the poet into limits too narrow for him to carry on and unravel his plot with propriety; because he is not allowed either sufficient time or space to display the passions of each character, so absolutely necessary to the completing of an opera, which, in the main, is nothing more than a tragic poem recited to musical sounds. And from the inconvenience alluded to here, it has happened that a great number of the French operas, as well as the first of the Italian, are nothing better than entertainments for the eyes, having more the appearance of a masquerade than of a regular dramatic performance; because therein the principal action is whelmed, as it were, under a heap of accessories, and, the poetical part being so flimsy and wretched, it was with just reason called a string of madrigals.

On the other hand, the subjects taken from history are liable to the objection of their not being so well adapted to music, which seems to exclude them from all plea of probability. This impleaded error may be observed every day upon the Italian stage. For who can be brought to think that the trillings of an air flow so justifiably from the mouth of a Julius Caesar or a Cato as from the lips of Venus or Apollo? Moreover, historical subjects do not furnish so striking a variety as those that are fabulous; they are apt to be too austere and monotonous. The stage, in such representations, would forever exhibit an almost solitary scene unless we are willing to number, among the ranks of actors, the mob of attendants that crowd after sovereigns, even into their closets. Besides, it is no easy matter to contrive ballets or interludes suitable to subjects taken from history; because all such entertainments ought to form a kind of social union and become, as it were, constituent parts of the whole. Such, for example, on the French stage, is the "Ballet of the Shepherds," that celebrates the marriage of Medoro with Angelica and makes Orlando acquainted with his accumulated wretchedness.[8] But this is far from being the effect of entertainments obtruded into the Italian operas, in which, although the subject be Roman and the ballet consist of dancers dressed like Roman soldiers, yet so unconnected is it with the business of the drama that the Scozzese or Furlana might as well be danced. And this is the reason why subjects chosen from history are for the most part necessitated to appear naked or to make use of such alien accoutrements as neither belong, nor are by any means suitable to them.

In order to obviate such inconveniences, the only means left to the poet is to exert all his judgement and taste in choosing the subject of his drama, that thereby he may attain his end, which is to delight the eyes and the ears, to rouse up and to affect the hearts of an audience, without the risk of sinning against reason or common sense. Wherefore the most prudent method he can adopt will be to make choice of an event that has happened, either in very remote times, or in countries very distant from us and quite estranged from our usages, which may afford various incidents of the marvellous, notwithstanding that the subject, at the same time, be extremely simple and not unknown, two desirable requisites.

The great distance of place where the action is fixed will prevent the recital of it to musical sounds from appearing quite so improbable to us. The marvellousness of the theme will furnish the author with an opportunity of interweaving therewith dances, choruses, and a variety of scenical decorations. The simplicity and notoriety of it will exempt his muse from the perplexing trouble and tedious preparations necessary to

---

8 In Lully's *Roland* (1685), II, v.

make the personages of a drama known, that, suitable to his notification, may be displayed their passions, the main spring and actuating spirit of the stage.

The two operas of *Didone* and *Achille in Sciro,* written by the celebrated Metastasio, come very near to the mark proposed here.[9] The subjects of these dramatic poems are simple and taken from very remote antiquity, but without being too far-fetched. In the midst of their most impassioned scenes, there is an opportunity of introducing splendid banquets, magnificent embassies, embarkations, choruses, battles, conflagrations, &c, so as to give a farther extension to the sovereignty of the musical drama, and makes its rightfulness be more ascertained than has been hitherto allowed.

The same doctrine may be advanced in regard to an opera on the subject of Montezuma, as much on account of the greatness, as of the novelty of such an action as that emperor's catastrophe must afford. A display of the Mexican and Spanish customs, seen for the first time together, must form a most beautiful contrast; and the barbaric magnificence of America would receive various heightenings by being opposed in different views to that of Europe.[a]

Several subjects may likewise be taken from Ariosto and Tasso, equally fitting as Montezuma for the opera theatre; for besides these being so universally known, they would furnish not only a fine field for exercising the passions, but also for introducing all the surprising illusions of the magic art.

An opera of Aeneas in Troy, or of Iphigenia in Aulis, would answer the same purpose;[10] and to the great variety for scenes and machinery, still greater heightenings might be derived from the enchanting *poetry* of Virgil and Euripides.

There are many other subjects to the full as applicable to the stage and that may be found equally fraught with marvellous incidents. Let then a poet who is judicious enough make a prudent collection of the subjects truly dramatic that are to be found in tracing the fabulous accounts of the heathen gods, and do the same also in regard to more modern times. Such

a Montezuma has been chosen for the subject of an opera, performed with the greatest magnificence at the Theatre Royal of Berlin. [Carl Heinrich Graun's *Montezuma,* a setting of G. P. Tagliazucchi's Italian version of a French libretto by Frederick the Great, was first performed on January 6, 1755, in Berlin. Algarotti signed the dedication of his *Saggio* on October 6, 1754. Yet this reference to the subject of Montezuma was surely written with the forthcoming performance in mind; Frederick had written to Algarotti about his plans for the opera as early as October 1753

(see his letter, quoted in part by Mayer-Reinach in his edition of the score for the *Denkmäler deutscher Tonkunst,* XV [1904]).—Ed.]

9 Metastasio's *Didone abbandonata* was first set to music by Domenico Sarro in 1724; the first setting of his *Achille in Sciro* (1736) was by Antonio Caldara.

10 Algarotti outlines an opera on the first of these subjects at the end of his *Saggio* and after this prints his own libretto on the second.

a proceeding, relative to the opera, would not be unlike what is oft-times found necessary in states, which it is impossible to preserve from decay and in the unimpaired enjoyment of their constitutional vigor without making them revert, from time to time, to their original principles.

2. ON THE MUSICAL COMPOSITION FOR OPERAS

No art now appears to stand so much in need of having the conclusive maxim of the preceding chapter put in practice as that of music, so greatly has it degenerated from its former dignity. For by laying aside every regard to decorum, and by scorning to keep within the bounds prescribed, it has suffered itself to be led far, very far astray in a bewildering pursuit of new-fangled whimsies and capricious conceits. Wherefore it would now be very seasonable to revive the decree made by the Lacedaemonians against that man who, through a distempered passion for novelty, had so sophisticated their music with his crotchety innovations that, from noble and manly, he rendered it effeminate and disgusting.

Mankind in general, it must be owned, are actuated by a love of novelty; and it is as true that, without it, music, like every other art, could not have received the great improvements it has. What we here implead is not a chaste passion for novelty, but a too great fondness for it; because it was that which reduced music to the declining state so much lamented by all true connoisseurs. While arts are in their infancy the love of novelty is no doubt essential, as it is to that they owe their being, and after, by its kindly influence, are improved, matured, and brought to perfection; but that point being once attained, the indulging this passion too far will, from benign and vivifying, become noxious and fatal. The arts have experienced this vicissitude in almost every nation where they have appeared, as, among the Italians, hath music at this time in a more remarkable manner.

On its revival in Italy, though in very barbarous times, this elegant art soon made its power be known throughout Europe; nay more, it was cultivated to such a degree by the tramontane nations that it may without exaggeration be asserted the Italians themselves were, for a certain period of time, glad to receive instructions from them.

On the return of music to Venice, Rome, Bologna, and Naples, as to its native place, such considerable improvements were made there in the musical art, during the two last centuries, that foreigners, in their turn, repaired thither for instruction; and such would be now the case were they not deterred from so doing by the raging frenzy after novelty that prevails in all the Italian schools. For, as if music were yet unrudimented and in its infancy, the mistaken professors spare no pains to trick out their art with every species of grotesque imagination and fantastical combination which they think can be executed by sounds. The public too, as if they were likewise in a state of childhood, change almost every moment their notions of, and fondness for things, rejecting today with scorn what yesterday was so passionately admired. The taste in singing, which, some years ago, enraptured audiences hung upon with wonder and delight, is now received with a supercilious disapprobation; not because it is sunk in real merit, but for the very groundless reason of its being old and not in frequent use. And thus we see that in compositions instituted for the representation of nature, whose mode is ever one, there is the same desire of changing as in the fluctuating fashions of the dresses we wear.

Another principal reason that can be assigned for the present degeneracy of music is the authority, power, and supreme command usurped in its name; because the composer, in consequence, acts like a despotic sovereign, contracting all the views of pleasing to his department alone. It is almost impossible to persuade him that he ought to be in a subordinate station, that music derives its greatest merit from being no more than an auxiliary, the handmaid to poetry. His chief business, then, is to predispose the minds of the audience for receiving the impression to be excited by the poet's verse, to infuse such a general tendency in their affections as to make them analogous with those particular ideas which the poet means to inspire. In fine, its genuine office is to communicate a more animating energy to the language of the muses.

That old and just charge, enforced by critics against operatical performances, of making their heroes and heroines die *singing*, can be ascribed to no other cause but the defect of a proper harmony between the words and the music. Were all ridiculous quavering omitted when the serious passions are to speak, and were the musical composition judiciously adapted to them, then it would not appear more improbable that a person should die singing, than reciting verses.

It is an undeniable fact that, in the earliest ages, the poets were all musical proficients; the vocal part, then, ranked as it should, which was to render the thoughts of the mind and affections of the heart with more forcible, more lively, and more kindling expression. But now that the twin sisters, poetry and music, go no longer hand in hand, it is not at all surprising, if the business of the one is to add coloring to what the other has designated, that the coloring, separately considered, appear beautiful; yet, upon a nice examination of the whole, the contours offend by not being properly rounded and by the absence of a social blending of the parts throughout. Nor can a remedy be applied to so great an evil otherwise but by the modest discretion of a composer who will not think it beneath him to receive, from the poet's mouth, the purport of his meaning and intention; who will also make himself a competent master of the author's sense before he writes a note of music and will ever afterwards confer with him concerning the music he shall have composed; and, by thus proceeding, keep up such a dependence and friendly intercourse as subsisted between Lully and Quinault, Vinci and Metastasio, which indeed the true regulation of an operatical theatre requires.

Among the errors observable in the present system of music, the most obvious, and that which first strikes the ears at the very opening of an opera, is the hackneyed manner of composing overtures, which are always made to consist of two allegros with one grave and to be as noisy as possible. Thus are they void of variation and so jog on much alike. Yet what a wide difference ought to be perceived between that, for example, which precedes the death of Dido and that which is prefixed to the nuptials of Demetrius and Cleonice. The main drift of an overture should be to announce, in a certain manner, the business of the drama and consequently prepare the audience to receive those affecting impressions that are to result from the whole of the performance, so that from hence a leading view and presaging notions of it may be conceived, as is of an oration from the exordium. But our present composers look upon an overture as an article quite detached and absolutely different from the poet's drama. They use it as an opportunity of playing off a tempestuous music to stun the ears of an audience. If some, however, employ it as an exordium, it is of a kindred complection to those of certain writers, who, with big and pompous words, repeatedly display before us the loftiness of the subject and the lowness of their genius; which preluding would suit any other subject as well and might as judiciously be prefixed for an exordium to one oration as another.[11]

After the overture, the next article that presents itself to our consideration is the recitative; and as it is wont to be the most noisy part of an opera, so is it the least attended to and the most neglected. It seems as if our musical composers were of opinion that the recitative is not of consequence enough to deserve their attention, they deeming it incapable of exciting any great delight. But the ancient masters thought in a quite different manner. There needs no stronger proof than to read what Jacopo Peri, who may be justly called the inventor of the recitative, wrote in his preface to *Euridice*.[12] When he had applied himself to an investigation of that

---

[11] Compare the criticism of Quantz (p. 14 above).   [12] See *S.R.* III, 13–16.

species of musical imitation which would the readiest lend itself to theatric exhibitions, he directed his tasteful researches to discover the manner which had been employed by the ancient Greeks on similar occasions. He carefully observed the Italian words which are capable of intonation or consonance and those which are not. He was very exact in minuting down our several modes of pronunciation, as well as the different accents of grief, of joy, and of all the other affections incident to the human frame, and that in order to make the bass move a timing attendance to them, now with more energy, now with less, according to the nature of each. So nicely scrupulous was he in his course of vocal experiments that he scrutinized intimately the very nature of the Italian language; on which account, in order to be more accurate, he frequently consulted with several gentlemen not less remarkable for the delicacy of their ears, than for their being uncommonly skilled both in the arts of music and poetry.

The final conclusion of his ingenious inquiry was that the groundwork of all such imitation should be an harmony chastely following nature step by step; a something between common speaking and melody; a well-combined system between that kind of performance which the ancients called the *diastematica*,[b] as if held in and suspended, and the other, called the *continuata*.[c] Such were the studies of the musical composers in former times. They proceeded in the improvement of their art with the utmost care and attention; and the effect proved that they did not lose their time in the pursuit of unprofitable subtleties.

The recitative in their time was made to vary with the subject and assume a complection suitable to the spirit of the words. It sometimes moved with a rapidity equal to that of the text and at others with an attendant slowness; but never failed to mark, in a conspicuous manner, those inflections and sallies which the violence of our passions can transfuse into the expression of them. All musical compositions finished in so masterly a manner were heard with delight. Numbers now living must remember how certain passages of simple recitative have affected the minds of an audience to a degree that no modern air is able to produce.

However, the recitative, all disregarded as it may be, has been known to excite emotions in an audience when it was of the *obbligato* kind, as the artists term it, that is, when strictly accompanied with instruments.[13] Per-

---

b Diastematic implies, according to the sense of the ancients, a simple interval, in opposition to a compound one, by them called a system. [Note from translator's glossary]

c Continuata, in vocal music, means to continue or hold on a sound with an equal strength or manner, or to continue a movement in an equal degree of time all the way. [Note from translator's glossary]

13 Compare the comments of Marcello (*S.R.* III. 69); for Metastasio's views, see his letter to Hasse, published by Burney in his *Memoirs of the Life and Writings of the Abate Metastasio* (London, 1796), I, 315-330.

haps it would not be improper to employ it oftener than is now the custom. What a kindly warmth might be communicated to the recitative if, where a passion exerts itself, it were to be enforced by the united orchestra! By so doing, the heart and mind at once would be stormed, as it were, by all the powers of music. A more evincing instance of such an effect cannot be quoted than the greater part of the last act of *Didone*, set to music by Vinci, which is executed in the taste recommended here; and no doubt but Virgil's self would be pleased to hear a composition so animating and so terrible.

Another good purpose which must be derived from such a practice is that then would not appear to us so enormous the great variety and disproportion now observable in the *andamento* of the recitative and that of the airs; but, on the contrary, a more friendly agreement among the several parts of an opera would be the result. The connoisseurs have often been displeased with those sudden transitions where, from a recitative in the *andantissimo* and gentlest movement, the performers are made to skip off and bound away into ariettas of the briskest execution, which is to the full as absurd as if a person, when soberly walking, should all on the sudden set to leaping and capering.

The surest method to bring about a better understanding among the several constituent parts of an opera would be not to crowd so much art into the airs and to curb the instrumental part more than is now the custom. In every period of the opera these two formed the most brilliant parts of it; and, in proportion as the musical composition has been more and more refined, so have they received still greater heightenings. They were naked formerly in comparison of what we see them now and were in as absolute a state of simplicity as they had been at their origin, insomuch that, either in point of melody or accompaniments, they did not rise above recitative.

Old Scarlatti was the first who infused life, movement, and spirit in them. It was he who clothed their nakedness with the splendid attire of noble accompaniments, but they were dealt out by him in a sober and judicious manner. They were by no means intricate or obscure, but open and obvious; highly finished, yet free from all the minuteness of affectation; and that not so much on account of the vastness of the theatres, by means of which many of the minor excellencies in musical performances may be lost, as in regard to the voices, to which alone they should be made subservient.

But unwarrantable changes have happened, since that great master's time down to ours, in which all the bounds of discretion are wantonly over-

leapt. The airs now are whelmed under and disfigured by crowded ornaments with which unnatural method the rage of novelty labors to embellish them. How tediously prolix are those *ritornelli* that precede them;
nay, and are often superfluous! For can anything be more improbable than
that, in an air expressive of wrath, an actor should calmly wait with his
hand stuck in his sword-belt until the *ritornello* be over to give vent to
a passion that is supposed to be boiling in his breast? And after the
ritornello then comes on the part to be sung, but the multitude of fiddles,
etc., that accompany it in general produce no better an effect than to
astonish the faculty of hearing and to drown the voice of a singer. Why
is there not more use made of the basses, and why not increase the number
of bass viols, which are the shades of music? Where is the necessity for
so many fiddles, with which our orchestras are now thronged? Fewer
would do, for they prove in this case like too many hands on board of a
ship which, instead of being assistant, are a great impediment to its navi-
gation. Why are not lutes and harps allowed a place? With their light
and piercing notes they would give a sprightliness to the *ripienos*. Why
is the *violetta* excluded from our orchestras, since from its institution it
was intended to act a middle part between the fiddles and the basses in
order that harmony might thence ensue?

But one of the most favorite practices now, and which indeed makes
our theatres to resound with peals of applause, is, in an air, to form a contest between the voice and a hautboy or between the voice and a trumpet
so as to exhibit, as it were, a kind of musical tilting-match with the utmost
exertion on either side. But such a skirmishing of voices and instruments is
very displeasing to the judicious part of the audience, who, on the contrary, would receive the greatest delight from the airs being accompanied
by instruments differently qualified from the present in use, and perhaps
even by the organ, as hath been formerly practiced.[d] The consequence
then would be that the respective qualities of instruments would be properly adapted to the nature of the words which they are intended to accompany and that they would aptly glide into those parts where a due
expression of the passion should stand most in need of them. Then the
accompaniment would be of service to the singer's voice by enforcing
the pathetic affections of the song and would prove not unlike to the
numbers of elegant and harmonious prose, which, according to the maxim
of a learned sage, ought to be like the beating on an anvil by smiths, at
once both musical and skilfully labored.

These faults, however considerable, are not the greatest that have been

---

[d] In the orchestra of the theatre in the famous villa of Cataio an organ is now to be seen.

introduced in the composition of airs; we must go farther back to investigate the first source of this evil, which, in the judgment of the most able professors, is to be found in the misconduct of choosing the subject of an air, because rarely any attention is paid to the *andamento* of the melody being natural and corresponding to the sense of the words it is to convey; besides, the extravagant varieties which it is now made to shift and turn about after cannot be managed to tend to one common center or point of unity. For the chief view of our present musical composers is to court, flatter, and surprise the ears, but not at all either to affect the heart or kindle the imagination of those who hear them; therefore, to accomplish their favorite end, they frequently bound over all rules. To be prodigal of shining passages, to repeat words without end, and musically to interweave or entangle them as they please are the three principal methods by which they carry on their operations.

The first of these expedients is indeed big with danger when we attend to the good effect that is to be expected from melody, because through its middle situation it possesses more of the *virtù*. Moreover, music delights to make an use of acute notes in her compositions, similar to that which painting does with striking lights in her performances.

In regard to brilliant passages, common sense forbids the introduction of them excepting where the words are expressive of passion or movement; otherwise they deserve no milder an appellation than being so many impertinent interruptions of the musical sense.

The repeating of words, and these chiming rencounters that are made for the sake of sound merely and are devoid of meaning, prove intolerable to a judicious ear. Words are to be treated in no other manner but according as the passion dictates; and, when the sense of an air is finished, the first part of it ought never to be sung over again, which is one of our modern innovations and quite repugnant to the natural process of our speech and passions, that are not accustomed to thus turn about and recoil upon themselves.

Most people who frequent our Italian theatres must have observed that, even when the sense of an air breathes a roused and furious tendency, yet, if the words "father" or "son" be in the text, the composer never fails to slacken his notes, to give them all the softness he can, and to stop in a moment the impetuosity of the tune. Moreover he flatters himself, on such an occasion, that, besides having clothed the words with sentimental sounds suitable to them, he hath also given to them an additional seasoning of variety.

But in our sense he hath entirely spoiled all with such a dissonance of

expression that will ever be objected to by all who have the least preten-
sions to judgment and taste. The duty of a composer is to express the sense,
not of this or that particular word, but the comprehensive meaning of all
the words in the air. It is also his duty to make variety flow from the
several modifications the subject in itself is capable of, and not from
adjuncts that adventitiously fasten themselves thereon and are foreign
from, preposterous, or repugnant to the poet's intention.

It seems that our composers take the same mistaken pains which some
writers do, who, regardless of connection and order in a discourse, bend
all their thoughts to collect and string together a number of finely sounding words. But, notwithstanding such words are ever so harmonious, a
discourse so written would prove an useless, vain, and contemptible performance. The same may be said of every musical composition which is
not calculated either to express some sentiment or awaken the idea of some
imagery of the mind.[e] Like what we have compared it to, it must turn out
but an useless and a vain production, which, should it be received with a
temporary and slight applause, must soon be consigned to perpetual
silence and oblivion, notwithstanding all the art that might have been
employed in choosing the musical combinations. On the contrary, those
airs alone remain forever engraven on the memory of the public that
paint images to the mind or express the passions, and are for that reason
called the speaking airs because more congenial to nature, which can never
be justly imitated but by a beautiful simplicity which will always bear
away the palm from the most labored refinements of art.

Although poetry and music be so near akin to each other, yet they have
pursued different views here in Italy. The muse presiding over harmony
was too chaste in the last century to give in to those affectations and lan-
guishing airs which she is at present so fond of indulging. She then knew
the way to the human heart and how to stamp permanent impressions
thereon; she possessed the secret of incorporating herself, as it were, with
the meaning of the words, and, that the probability might seem the
greater, she was to the last degree simple, yet affecting, though at the same
time the poetic muse had run away from all semblance of truth to make
a parade of hyperbolical, far-fetched, fantastical whimsies. Since that time,
by a strange vicissitude, as soon as poetry was made to return into the
right path, music ran astray.

Such excellent masters as a Cesti and a Carissimi had the hard fate of

---

e "All music that paints nothing is only noise,
and, were it not for custom that unnatures everything, it would excite no more pleasure than a
sequel of harmonious and finely sounding words
without any order or connection."—Preface of
the *Encyclopédie*. [Algarotti's quotation is from
the "Discours préliminaire" of d'Alembert.—Ed.]

composing music for words in the style of Achillino,[14] men who were equal to the noble task of conveying in musical numbers the sighs and love-breathings of a Petrarch. But now, alas, the elegant, the terse, the graceful poems of Metastasio are degraded into music by wretched composers. It must not, however, be hence concluded that no vestige of true music is to be perceived among us, because, as a proof against such an opinion, and that no small one, may be produced our intermezzi and comic operas, wherein the first of all musical requisites, that of expression, takes the lead more than in any other of our compositions; which is owing perhaps to the impossibility the masters found of indulging their own fancy in a wanton display of all the secrets of their art and the manifold treasures of musical knowledge, from which ostentatious prodigality they were luckily prevented by the very limited abilities of their singers. Wherefore, in their own despite, they found themselves obliged to cultivate simplicity and follow nature. Whatever may have been the cause, this style soon obtained the vogue and triumphed over every other although called plebeian.

To this kind of performance we owe the extending of our musical fame on the other side of the Alps among the French, who had been at all times our rivals in every polite art. The emulous contention which had so long subsisted between them and us for a pre-eminence in music is universally known. No means could be hit on by our artists to make their execution agreeable to Gallic ears, and the Italian melody was abhorred by them as much as had been, in former times, an Italian regency.

But no sooner was heard upon the theatre of Paris the natural yet elegant style of the *Serva padrona*,[15] rich with airs so expressive and duets so pleasing, than the far greater part of the French became not only proselytes to, but even zealous advocates in behalf of the Italian music. A revolution so sudden was caused by an intermezzo and two comic actors. The like had been attempted in vain in the most elaborate pieces of eminent composers through a long series of years, although bedizened over with so many brilliant passages, surprising shakes, etc. Nor did the repeated efforts of our most celebrated performers, vocal or instrumental, fare better.

Nevertheless, all the good musical composition modern Italy can boast of is not absolutely confined to the intermezzi and comic operas, for it must be confessed that in some of our late serious pieces there are parts not unworthy of the best masters and the most applauded era of music. Several

---

14 G. F. Achillini (1466–1538), prolific author of pedantic verse. 15 See p. 56 above, note 20.

instances are to be found in the works of Pergolesi and Vinci, whom death too soon snatched from us, as well as in those of Galuppi, Jommelli, "Il Sassone," [16] that are deserving to be for ever in esteem.

Through the energy of the composition of these masters, music makes an audience feel sometimes from the stage the very same effects that were formerly felt in the chapels under the direction of Palestrina and Rodio.[17] We have likewise proofs of the like powerful influence in the skilful productions of Benedetto Marcello, a man second in merit to none among the ancients and certainly the first among the moderns. Who ever was more animated with a divine flame in conceiving and more judicious in conducting his works than Marcello? In the cantatas of Timotheus and Cassandra and in the celebrated collection of psalms [18] he hath expressed in a wonderful manner, not only all the different passions of the heart, but even the most delicate sentiments of the mind. He has, moreover, the art of representing to our fancy things even inanimate. He found out the secret of associating with all the gracefulness and charms of the modern the chaste correctness of ancient music, which in him appears like the attractive graces of a beloved and respected matron.

16 Johann Adolph Hasse.

17 Rocco Rodio, a Neapolitan composer of the sixteenth century and the author of a treatise, *Regole di musica*, published in 1609.

18 Marcello's "Timoteo" (1726) has the sub-title "Gli effetti della musica"; the four volumes of his *Estro poetico-armonico*, collected settings of fifty paraphrases from the Psalms, were first published in Venice from 1724 to 1727.

7. C. W. von Gluck

Born in 1714 near the German-Bohemian border, Gluck is the master who liberated the opera from the conventions of contemporary Italian *opera seria* and created a new operatic style based on truly dramatic expression. After studying for four years with Sammartini in Milan and visiting London and various cities on the Continent, Gluck settled in Vienna in 1750.

The opera *Orfeo ed Euridice*, written in 1762, marks a turning point in Gluck's career. Here he applied for the first time his new ideas, supported by his able and original librettist, Ranieri de' Calzabigi. Gluck gives an explanation of his aims in the forewords to the printed scores of his operas *Alceste* (1768) and *Paride ed Elena* (1770). In 1772, Gluck found a new and congenial collaborator in Le Bland Du Roullet, who had adapted Racine's *Iphigénie* as an opera libretto. The new score—*Iphigénie en Aulide*—was accepted by the Paris Opéra, and Gluck himself went to Paris to direct the rehearsals. After reinforcing his position with *Armide* (1777) and *Iphigénie en Tauride* (1779), Gluck returned, crowned with fresh laurels, to Vienna, where he died in 1787.

Alceste [1]

[*1769*]

Dedication

YOUR ROYAL HIGHNESS:

WHEN I undertook to write the music for *Alceste*, I resolved to divest it entirely of all those abuses, introduced into it either by the mistaken vanity of singers or by the too great complaisance of composers, which have so

1 Text: As translated by Eric Blom for Alfred Einstein's *Gluck* (London, J. M. Dent & Sons, Ltd., 1936), pp. 98–100.

long disfigured Italian opera and made of the most splendid and most beautiful of spectacles the most ridiculous and wearisome. I have striven to restrict music to its true office of serving poetry by means of expression and by following the situations of the story, without interrupting the action or stifling it with a useless superfluity of ornaments; and I believed that it should do this in the same way as telling colors affect a correct and well-ordered drawing, by a well-assorted contrast of light and shade, which serves to animate the figures without altering their contours. Thus I did not wish to arrest an actor in the greatest heat of dialogue in order to wait for a tiresome *ritornello*, nor to hold him up in the middle of a word on a vowel favorable to his voice, nor to make display of the agility of his fine voice in some long-drawn passage, nor to wait while the orchestra gives him time to recover his breath for a cadenza. I did not think it my duty to pass quickly over the second section [2] of an aria of which the words are perhaps the most impassioned and important, in order to repeat regularly four times over those of the first part, and to finish the aria where its sense may perhaps not end for the convenience of the singer who wishes to show that he can capriciously vary a passage in a number of guises; in short, I have sought to abolish all the abuses against which good sense and reason have long cried out in vain.

I have felt that the overture ought to apprise the spectators of the nature of the action that is to be represented and to form, so to speak, its argument; that the concerted instruments should be introduced in proportion to the interest and the intensity of the words, and not leave that sharp contrast between the aria and the recitative in the dialogue, so as not to break a period unreasonably nor wantonly disturb the force and heat of the action.

Furthermore, I believed that my greatest labor should be devoted to seeking a beautiful simplicity, and I have avoided making displays of difficulty at the expense of clearness; nor did I judge it desirable to discover novelties if it was not naturally suggested by the situation and the expression; and there is no rule which I have not thought it right to set aside willingly for the sake of an intended effect.

Such are my principles. By good fortune my designs were wonderfully furthered by the libretto, in which the celebrated author, devising a new dramatic scheme, for florid descriptions, unnatural paragons, and

---

2 By "second section" Gluck means the central or contrasting section of the da capo aria. In the eighteenth century the first section of such an aria regularly presented its full text twice and had then to be repeated after the central or con- trasting section, hence Gluck's reference to repeating the words of the first part "four times over." Frederick the Great says much the same thing in a letter of May 4, 1754, quoted in *Denkmäler der Tonkunst in Österreich*, XV (1904), ix.

sententious, cold morality, had substituted heartfelt language, strong passions, interesting situations and an endlessly varied spectacle. The success of the work justified my maxims, and the universal approbation of so enlightened a city has made it clearly evident that simplicity, truth and naturalness are the great principles of beauty in all artistic manifestations. For all that, in spite of repeated urgings on the part of some most eminent persons to decide upon the publication of this opera of mine in print, I was well aware of all the risk run in combating such firmly and profoundly rooted prejudices, and I thus felt the necessity of fortifying myself with the most powerful patronage of YOUR ROYAL HIGHNESS, whose August Name I beg you may have the grace to prefix to this my opera, a name which with so much justice enjoys the suffrages of an enlightened Europe. The great protector of the fine arts, who reigns over a nation that had the glory of making them arise again from universal oppression and which itself has produced the greatest models, in a city that was always the first to shake off the yoke of vulgar prejudices in order to clear a path for perfection, may alone undertake the reform of that noble spectacle in which all the fine arts take so great a share. If this should succeed, the glory of having moved the first stone will remain for me, and in this public testimonial of Your Highness's furtherance of the same, I have the honor to subscribe myself, with the most humble respect,

Your Royal Highness's

Most humble, most devoted, and most obliged servant,

CHRISTOFORO GLUCK.

8. F. L. Du Roullet

Du Roullet was the young dilettante who adapted Racine's *Iphigénie* as an opera libretto for Gluck. His *Lettre à M. D., un des directeurs de l'Opéra de Paris* (1772) was reprinted in 1781, together with other writings called forth by the dispute between the partisans of Gluck and Piccinni, in *Mémoires pour servir à l'histoire de la révolution opérée dans la musique par M. le Chevalier Gluck*, by Gaspard Leblond.

Letter to M. d'Auvergne [1]

[*1722*]

Vienna in Austria, August 1, 1772

THE ESTEEM which is due to you, Sir,[2] both for your talents, certainly most distinguished, and for the uprightness of your character, with which I am particularly acquainted, has determined me to undertake to write to you, to inform you that the famous M. Glouch,[3] so well known throughout Europe, has composed a French opera which he would like to have given upon the Paris stage. This great man, after composing more than forty Italian operas, which have had the greatest success in all the theatres where that language is accepted, has been convinced by a thoughtful reading of the ancients and the moderns and by profound meditations upon his art that the Italians, in their theatrical compositions, have strayed from the true path; that the French style is the true style of musical drama; that if it has not yet attained to perfection, the reason must be sought less in the talents of French musicians than in the authors of the poems, who, entirely unacquainted with the scope of musical art, have in their composi-

---

1 Text: *Mercure de France*, Octobre 1772, pp. 169–174.

2 The Chevalier Antoine d'Auvergne.

3 Du Roullet uses this spelling throughout.

tions preferred wit to sentiment, gallantry to the passions, and sweetness and color of versification to the pathetic in style and in character.

In accordance with these reflections, having communicated his ideas to a man of much wit, talent, and taste,[4] he obtained from him two Italian poems which he set to music. He has himself directed these two operas in the theaters of Parma, Milan, Naples, etc. They have had incredible success there and have produced a revolution in this kind of work in Italy. Last winter, in M. Glouch's absence, the city of Bologna presented one of these operas, and when the proceeds were reckoned, Bologna had made by this production more than 80,000 ducats, about 900,000 French livres.[5] Upon his return here, M. Glouch, enlightened by his own experience, believed himself to have perceived that the Italian language, better adapted by its frequent repetition of vowels to what the Italians call passages, lacks the clearness and the energy of French; that the advantage which we have been conceding to the former was even destructive of the true musical-dramatic style, in which every passage is an anomaly or at least weakens the expression.

In accordance with these observations M. Glouch became indignant at the bold assertions of those of our French writers who have dared to calumniate the French language by maintaining that it is incapable of lending itself to great musical composition.[6] No one can be a more competent judge in this matter than M. Glouch; he has a perfect knowledge of the two languages; and although he speaks French with difficulty, he has made a special and thorough study of it. In short, he knows all its fine distinctions and especially its prosody, which he observes most scrupulously. For a long time he has been making trial of his skill in dealing with these two languages in works in different styles, and has won successes at a court where they are equally familiar, although for practical use French is preferred, at a court the better prepared to judge of talents of this kind because the ear and the taste are there constantly exercised.

After he had made these observations, M. Glouch was desirous of an opportunity of supporting his judgment in favor of the French language by a practical demonstration, when chance caused the tragedy-opera *Iphigénie en Aulide* to fall into his hands. He believed that in this work he had found what he was seeking. The author, or to speak more exactly, the adapter of this poem [7] seems to me to have followed Racine with the most scrupulous attention. It is his *Iphigénie* itself, converted into an

---

4 Ranieri de' Calzabigi, author of *Orfeo ed Euridice* (1762) and *Alceste* (1767), also of *Paride ed Elena* (1770).

5 There is no mention of any such performance in Loewenberg's *Annals.*

6 Particularly Jean Jacques Rousseau.

7 Du Roullet himself.

opera. To attain this result it was necessary to simplify the exposition and to eliminate the episode of Ériphyle. Calchas is introduced into the first act instead of the confidant Arcas; by this device the exposition is given by means of action, the subject is simplified, and the action, more closely knit, advances more rapidly to its goal. The interest has not been diminished by these changes; it has even seemed to me as complete as the tragedy of Racine. Since after the episode of Ériphyle had been removed the denouement of the play of this great man could no longer serve for the opera in question, it has been replaced by a denouement in action which should produce a very good effect, and of which the idea has been furnished to the author by the Greek tragic writers, as well as by Racine himself in the preface to his *Iphigénie*.[8]

The whole work has been divided into three acts, a division which seems to me to be the most favorable for the kind of work which calls for great rapidity of action. In each act the author has naturally introduced a brilliant *divertissement*, derived without effort from the subject and so connected with it as to seem one of its parts, which augments or completes the action. He has taken great pains to oppose situation to situation and character to character, producing thereby a piquant variety, necessary to hold the spectator's attention and to interest him throughout the duration of the performance. He has found a means of presenting a noble and magnificent spectacle to the eye without resorting to machines and without requiring considerable expenditure. I do not believe that any one has ever produced a new opera which called for less expense and was at the same time more imposing.

The author of this poem, of which the entire performance, including the *divertissements*, ought to take at the most no longer than two and a half hours, has made it his obligation to use the thoughts and even the lines of Racine when the nature of the work, although different, has allowed. The subject of *Iphigénie en Aulide* has seemed to me so much the better chosen in that the author, by following Racine as closely as possible, has made sure of the effect of his work, and that by the certainty of success he is amply compensated for whatever he may have lost on the side of self-esteem.

M. Glouch's name alone would absolve me, Sir, from speaking of the music of this opera, if the pleasure it has given me on repeated hearing permitted me to remain silent. It seemed to me that this great man has in this composition exhausted all the resources of his art. Simple, natural

---

[8] What Racine actually does in his preface is to report the classical tradition for Diana's intervention and to reject this ending as too absurd and incredible for the theater of his time.

song, always guided by the truest, the most affecting expression and by the most ingratiating melody; an inexhaustible variety in his subject and in his turn of phrase; the grandest effects of harmony, employed equally in the terrible, the pathetic, and the graceful; a recitative that is rapid, yet noble and expressive of the style; airs for dances of the greatest variety, in a new style and of the most agreeable freshness; choruses, duets, trios, quartets equally expressive, touching, and well-declaimed; the prosody of the language scrupulously observed—everything in this composition seemed to me to be in our style; nothing seemed foreign to my French ear; it is the work of a talent; everywhere M. Glouch is poet and musician; everywhere in it one recognizes the man of genius and at the same time the man of taste; nothing in it is weak or neglected.

You know, Sir, that I am not an enthusiast, and that in the quarrels which have arisen concerning the preference between the musical styles I have preserved an absolute neutrality. I consequently flatter myself that you will not be prejudiced against the eulogy which I am here bestowing on the music of the opera of *Iphigénie*. I am convinced that you will be eager to applaud. I know that no one desires more than you the progress of your art, to which you have already greatly contributed by your productions and by the applause which I have seen you give to those who distinguished themselves therein. You will therefore be pleased, both as a man of talent and as a good citizen, to see a foreigner as famous as M. Glouch employed in working in our language and in avenging it, in the eyes of all Europe, of the calumnious imputations of our own authors.

M. Glouch desires to know whether the management of the Académie de Musique would have enough confidence in his talents to decide to give his opera. He is ready to make the journey to France, but wishes to be assured in advance both that his opera will be represented and at what time, approximately, this can take place.

If you have nothing determined on for the winter, for Lent, or for the reopening after Easter, I believe that you could not do better than to assign him one of those periods. M. Glouch has been most pressingly invited to Naples for the month of May; he has been unwilling to make any engagement in that quarter, and is resolved to sacrifice the profits which are offered him if he can be assured that his opera will be accepted by your Academy, to which I beg you to transmit this letter, and to send me word of the decision which will fix that of M. Glouch. I should be greatly flattered to share with you, Sir, the distinction of making known to our nation all that it can promise itself to the advantage of its language embellished by the art which you profess. With these sentiments I am, Sir,

Your very humble and obedient servant.

P. S. If the management has not enough confidence in the opinion which I have formed of the words of the opera, I will send it to you on the first occasion.

I forgot to tell you, Sir, that M. Glouch, very disinterested by nature, does not ask for his work more than the sum fixed by the management for the authors of new operas.

9. C. W. von Gluck

Letter to the Editor of the "Mercure de France"[1]
[*1773*]

Sir:

I SHOULD be liable to just reproaches and I should bring very serious reproaches against myself if after reading the letter, written from here to one of the directors of the Académie Royale de Musique, which you published in the *Mercure* of last October and of which the opera *Iphigénie* is the subject; if, I say, after testifying to my gratitude to the author of that letter for the praises which he has been pleased to lavish upon me, I did not hasten to declare that his friendship and a prejudice too greatly in my favor have without doubt carried him away and that I am very far from flattering myself that I deserve the eulogies which he bestows on me. I should bring against myself a still graver reproach if I permitted the attribution to myself of the invention of a new style of Italian opera of which the success has justified the endeavor. It is to M. de Calzabigi that the principal merit belongs; and if my music has had a certain éclat, I believe that I must recognize that it is to him that I am indebted for it, since it is he who has made it possible for me to develop the resources of my art. This author, full of genius and talent, has in his poems of *Orfeo*, of *Alceste*, and of *Paride* followed a path little known to the Italians. These works are filled with those happy situations, those terrible and pathetic strokes, which furnish to the composer the means of expressing the great passions and of creating a music energetic and touching. Whatever the talent of the composer, he will never compose any but mediocre music if the poet does not arouse in him that enthusiasm without which the productions of all the arts are feeble and languid; the imitation of nature is by general agreement their common object. It is this which I

1 Text: *Mercure de France*, Février 1773, pp. 182–184.

seek to attain. Always simple and natural, so far as is within my power, my music is directed only to the greatest expression and to the reinforcement of the declamation of the poetry.

This is the reason why I never employ the trills, the passages, or the cadenzas of which the Italians are profuse. Their language, which easily lends itself to them, has therefore in this respect no advantage for me. It has without doubt many others; but, born in Germany, whatever study I have been able to make of the Italian language, as well as of the French, I do not believe that it is permitted to me to appreciate the delicate distinctions which can give the preference to one of the two, and I think that every foreigner should abstain from judging between them. But what I believe it is permitted me to say is that the one which will always suit me the best is the one in which the poet will furnish me the greatest number of different means of expressing the passions. This is the advantage which I believe I have found in the words of the opera *Iphigénie*, of which the poetry had seemed to me to have all the energy proper to inspire me to good music.

Although I have never had occasion to offer my works to any theater, I cannot bear ill will to the author of the letter to one of the Directors for having proposed my *Iphigénie* to your Académie de Musique. I admit that I should have produced it in Paris with pleasure, since by its effect and with the aid of the famous M. Rousseau of Geneva, whom I was planning to consult, we might perhaps together have been able, by searching for a melody noble, affecting, and natural, with an exact declamation according to the prosody of each language and the character of each people, to determine the means which I have in view of producing a music suitable for all the nations and of causing the ridiculous distinctions of national music to disappear.[2] The study which I have made of the works on music of that great man, among others the letter in which he analyzes the monologue in Lully's *Armide*,[3] proves the sublimity of his attainments and the sureness of his taste, and has filled me with admiration. From it I have retained the profound conviction that if he had chosen to apply himself to the practice of that art, he would have been able to accomplish in reality the marvelous effects which antiquity attributed to music. I am charmed to find here the opportunity of rendering to him publicly the tribute of praise which I believe him to merit.

---

2 This is in direct and deliberate contrast to the reference to Rousseau in Du Roullet's letter. Rousseau's opinion of Gluck's music is set forth at some length in his "Fragmens d'observations sur l'*Alceste* italien de M. le Chevalier Gluck,"

appended to a letter of his to Dr. Burney and included in most editions of his writings on music.
3 See above, pp. 64–80, where Rousseau's analysis is, however, omitted.

I pray, Sir, that you will consent to insert this letter in your next *Mercure.*

I have the honor to be, etc.

Chevalier Gluck

IV

The European Scene

10. Charles Burney

Born in 1726, Burney was appointed organist at St. Dionis-Backchurch, London, in 1749 and in 1769 received the degrees of Mus.Bac. and Mus.Doc. from Oxford University. Following this, Burney made extensive studies and journeys to the Continent to assemble the materials for his general history of music. In 1770 he went for this purpose to France and Italy; a trip to the Low Countries, Germany, and Austria followed in 1772.

The impressions gathered in the course of these tours are set down in two valuable books: *The Present State of Music in France and Italy* (1771), and *The Present State of Music in Germany, the Netherlands and United Provinces* (1773). The first volume of Burney's *General History of Music* appeared in 1776, but it was not until 1789 that the fourth and final volume was published. Burney also wrote a number of books of lesser importance, among them a biography of Metastasio, the librettist, and an *Account of the Musical Performances in Westminster Abbey in Commemoration of Handel* (1785). He died in 1814.

From The Present State of Music in France and Italy [1]

[*1771*]

Naples

I ENTERED this city, impressed with the highest ideas of the perfect state in which I should find practical music. It was at Naples only that I expected to have my ears gratified with every musical luxury and refinement which Italy could afford. My visits to other places were in the way of *business*, for the performance of a *task* I had assigned myself; [2] but I

1 Text: The original edition (London, 1771), pp. 291–293, 298–304, 305–307, 316–319, 324–330, 335–340, 352–358.

2 The collection of materials for his *General History of Music*.

came hither animated by the hope of pleasure. And what lover of music could be in the place which had produced the two Scarlattis, Vinci, Leo, Pergolesi, Porpora, Farinelli, Jommelli, Piccinni, and innumerable others of the first eminence among composers and performers, both vocal and instrumental, without the most sanguine expectations. How far these expectations were gratified, the reader will find in the course of my narrative, which is constantly a faithful transcript of my feelings at the time I entered them in my journal, immediately after hearing and seeing, with a mind not conscious of any prejudice or partiality.

I arrived here about five o'clock in the evening, on Tuesday, October 16,[3] and at night went to the Teatro de'Fiorentini to hear the comic opera of *Gelosia per gelosia,* set to music by Signor Piccinni. This theatre is as small as Mr. Foote's in London,[4] but higher, as there are five rows of boxes in it. Notwithstanding the court was at Portici, and a great number of families at their *villeggiature,* or country houses, so great is the reputation of Signor Piccinni, that every part of the house was crowded. Indeed this opera had nothing else but the merit and reputation of the composer to support it, as both the drama and singing were bad. There was, however, a comic character performed by Signor Casaccia, a man of infinite humor; the whole house was in a roar the instant he appeared; and the pleasantry of this actor did not consist in buffoonery, nor was it local, which in Italy, and, indeed, elsewhere, is often the case; but was of that original and general sort as would excite laughter at all times and in all places.

The airs of this burletta are full of pretty passages, and, in general, most ingeniously accompanied: there was no dancing, so that the acts, of which there were three, seemed rather long.

*   *   *   *   *

Thursday 18. I was very happy to find, upon my arrival at Naples, that though many persons to whom I had letters were in the country, yet Signor Jommelli and Signor Piccinni were in town. Jommelli was preparing a serious opera for the great theatre of S. Carlo, and Piccinni had just brought the burletta on the stage which I have mentioned before.

This morning I visited Signor Piccinni, and had the pleasure of a long conversation with him. He seems to live in a reputable way, has a good house, and many servants and attendants about him. He is not more than four or five and forty; looks well, has a very animated countenance, and

---

is a polite and agreeable little man, though rather grave in his manner for a Neapolitan possessed of so much fire and genius. His family is rather numerous; one of his sons is a student in the University of Padua. After reading a letter which Mr. Giardini [5] was so obliging as to give me to him, he told me he should be extremely glad if he could be of any use either to me or my work. My first enquiries were concerning the Neapolitan conservatorios; for he having been brought up in one of them himself, his information was likely to be authentic and satisfactory. In my first visit I confined my questions chiefly to the four following subjects:

1. The antiquity of these establishments.
2. Their names.
3. The number of masters and scholars.
4. The time for admission, and for quitting these schools.

To my first demand he answered that the conservatorios were of ancient standing, as might be seen by the ruinous condition of one of the buildings, which was ready to tumble down.[a]

To my second, that their names were S. Onofrio, La Pietà, and S. Maria di Loreto.

To my third question he answered that the number of scholars in the first conservatorio is about ninety, in the second a hundred and twenty, and in the other, two hundred.

That each of them has two principal *maestri di cappella,* the first of whom superintends and corrects the compositions of the students; the second the singing and gives lessons. That there are assistant masters, who are called *maestri secolari;* one for the violin, one for the violoncello, one for the harpsichord, one for the hautbois, one for the French horn, and so for other instruments.

To my fourth inquiry he answered that boys are admitted from eight or ten to twenty years of age; that when they are taken in young they are bound for eight years; but, when more advanced, their admission is difficult, except they have made a considerable progress in the study and practice of music. That after boys have been in a conservatorio for some years, if no genius is discovered, they are dismissed to make way for others. That some are taken in as pensioners, who pay for their teaching; and others, after having served their time out, are retained to teach the rest; but that in both these cases they are allowed to go out of the conservatorio at pleasure.

a I afterwards obtained, from good authority, the exact date of each of these foundations; their fixed and stated rules, amounting to thirty-one; and the orders given to the rectors for regulating the conduct and studies of the boys, every month in the year.

5 Felice de Giardini, an Italian composer and violinist resident in London.

I inquired throughout Italy at what place boys were chiefly qualified for singing by castration, but could get no certain intelligence. I was told at Milan that it was at Venice; at Venice that it was at Bologna; but at Bologna the fact was denied, and I was referred to Florence; from Florence to Rome, and from Rome I was sent to Naples. The operation most certainly is against law in all these places, as well as against nature; and all the Italians are so much ashamed of it that in every province they transfer it to some other.

> Ask where's the North? at York, 'tis on the Tweed;
> In Scotland, at the Orcades; and there,
> At Greenland, Zembla, or the Lord knows where.
> —Pope, *Essay on Man.*

However, with respect to the conservatorios at Naples, Mr. Gemineau, the British consul, who has so long resided there and who has made very particular inquiries, assured me, and his account was confirmed by Dr. Cirillo, an eminent and learned Neapolitan physician, that this practice is absolutely forbidden in the conservatorios, and that the young *castrati* come from Leccia in Apuglia; but, before the operation is performed, they are brought to a conservatorio to be tried as to the probability of voice, and then are taken home by their parents for this barbarous purpose. It is, however, death by the laws to all those who perform the operation, and excommunication to everyone concerned in it, unless it be done, as is often pretended, upon account of some disorders which may be supposed to require it, and with the consent of the boy. And there are instances of its being done even at the request of the boy himself, as was the case of the Grassetto at Rome.[6] But as to these previous trials of the voice, it is my opinion that the cruel operation is but too frequently performed without trial, or at least without sufficient proofs of an improvable voice; otherwise such r umbers could never be found in every great town throughout Italy, without any voice at all, or at least without one sufficient to compensate such a loss. Indeed all the *musici* [b] in the churches at present are made up of the refuse of the opera houses, and it is very rare to meet with a tolerable voice upon the establishment in any church throughout Italy. The virtuosi who sing there occasionally, upon great festivals only, are usually strangers, and paid by the time.

·   ·   ·   ·   ·

---

bThe word *musico*, in Italy, seems now wholly appropriated to a singer with a soprano or contralto voice, which has been preserved by art.

6 "*Il Grassetto*, a boy who submitted to mutilation by his own choice and against the advice of his friends for the preservation of his voice, which is indeed a very good one." (Burney)

From hence I went directly to the comic opera, which, tonight,[7] was at the Teatro Nuovo. This house is not only less than the Fiorentini, but is older and more dirty. The way to it, for carriages, is through streets very narrow, and extremely inconvenient. This burletta was called the *Trame per Amore,* and set by Signor Giovanni Paesiello, *Maestro di Cappella Napolitano.* The singing was but indifferent; there were nine characters in the piece, and yet not one good voice among them; however, the music pleased me very much; it was full of fire and fancy, the ritornelles abounding in new passages, and the vocal parts in elegant and simple melodies, such as might be remembered and carried away after the first hearing, or be performed in private by a small band, or even without any other instrument than a harpsichord.[e] The overture, of one movement only, was quite comic, and contained a perpetual succession of pleasant passages. There was no dancing, which made it necessary to spin the acts out to rather a tiresome length. The airs were much applauded, though it was the fourteenth representation of the opera. The author was engaged to compose for Turin, at the next carnival, for which place he set out while I was at Naples. The performance began about a quarter before eight, and continued till past eleven o'clock.

. . . . .

Friday 26. This morning I first had the pleasure of seeing and conversing with Signor Jommelli, who arrived at Naples from the country but the night before. He is extremely corpulent, and, in the face, not unlike what I remember Handel to have been, yet far more polite and soft in his manner. I found him in his night-gown, at an instrument, writing. He received me very politely, and made many apologies for not having called on me, in consequence of a card I had left at his house; but apologies were indeed unnecessary, as he was but just come to town, and at the point of bringing out a new opera that must have occupied both his time and thoughts sufficiently. He had heard of me from Mr. Hamilton.[8] I gave him Padre Martini's letter, and after he had read it we went to business directly. I told him my errand to Italy, and showed him my plan, for I knew his time was precious. He read it with great attention, and conversed very openly and rationally; said the part I had undertaken was much

---

e This is seldom the case in modern opera songs, so crowded is the score and the orchestra. Indeed Piccinni is accused of employing instruments to such excess, that in Italy no copyist will transcribe one of his operas without being paid a zechin more than for one by any other composer. But in burlettas he has generally bad voices to write for, and is obliged to produce all his effects with instruments; and, indeed, this kind of drama usually abounds with brawls and *squabbles,* which it is necessary to enforce with the orchestra.

7 The date is still October 18.

8 The British Minister to the Court of Naples.

neglected at present in Italy; that the conservatorios, of which, I told him, I wished for information, were now at a low ebb, though formerly so fruitful in great men. He mentioned to me a person of great learning who had been translating David's Psalms into excellent Italian verse; in the course of which work he had found it necessary to write a dissertation on the music of the ancients, which he had communicated to him. He said this writer was a fine and subtle critic; had differed in several points from Padre Martini; had been in correspondence with Metastasio, and had received a long letter from him on the subject of lyric poetry and music; all of which he thought necessary for me to see. He promised to procure me the book, and to make me acquainted with the author.[9] He spoke very much in praise of Alessandro Scarlatti, as to his church music, such as motets, masses, and oratorios; promised to procure me information concerning the conservatorios, and whatever else was to my purpose, and in his power. He took down my direction, and assured me that the instant he had got his opera [10] on the stage he should be entirely at my service. Upon my telling him that my time for remaining at Naples was very short, that I should even then have been on the road on my way home but for his opera, which I so much wished to hear; that besides urgent business in England, there was great probability of a war, which would keep me a prisoner on the continent: he, in answer to that, and with great appearance of sincerity, said, if after I returned to England anything of importance to my plan occurred, he would not fail of sending it to me. In short, I went away in high good humor with this truly great composer, who is indisputably one of the first of his profession now alive in the universe; for were I to name the living composers of Italy for the stage, according to my idea of their merit, it would be in the following order: Jommelli, Galuppi, Piccinni, and Sacchini. It is, however, difficult to decide which of the two composers first mentioned has merited most from the public; Jommelli's works are full of great and noble ideas, treated with taste and learning; Galuppi's abound in fancy, fire, and feeling; Piccinni has far surpassed all his contemporaries in the comic style; and Sacchini seems the most promising composer in the serious.

·   ·   ·   ·   ·

---

9 Saverio Mattei, whose biography of Metastasio was published in 1785. For Metastasio's letters to him see Burney's *Memoirs of the Life and Writings of the Abate Metastasio* (London, 1796), II, 378–420; III, 115–153.

10 His *Demofoonte;* see above, p. 688, and below, pp. 694–696. Actually, this was an old work; first performed in Padua on June 16, 1743, it had already been heard in London, Milan, and Stuttgart.

Wednesday, October 31. This morning I went with young Oliver [11] to his conservatorio of S. Onofrio, and visited all the rooms where the boys practise, sleep, and eat. On the first flight of stairs was a trumpeter, screaming upon his instrument till he was ready to burst; on the second was a French horn, bellowing in the same manner. In the common practising room there was a "Dutch concert," consisting of seven or eight harpsichords, more than as many violins, and several voices, all performing different things, and in different keys: other boys were writing in the same room; but it being holiday time, many were absent who usually study and practise in this room. The jumbling them all together in this manner may be convenient for the house, and may teach the boys to attend to their own parts with firmness, whatever else may be going forward at the same time; it may likewise give them force, by obliging them to play loud in order to hear themselves; but in the midst of such jargon, and continued dissonance, it is wholly impossible to give any kind of polish or finishing to their performance; hence the slovenly coarseness so remarkable in their public exhibitions; and the total want of taste, neatness, and expression in all these young musicians, till they have acquired them elsewhere.

The beds, which are in the same room, serve for seats to the harpsichords and other instruments. Out of thirty or forty boys who were practising, I could discover but two that were playing the same piece; some of those who were practising on the violin seemed to have a great deal of hand. The violoncellos practise in another room; and the flutes, oboes, and other wind instruments in a third, except the trumpets and horns, which are obliged to fag, either on the stairs, or on the top of the house.

There are in this college sixteen young *castrati*, and these lie upstairs, by themselves, in warmer apartments than the other boys, for fear of colds, which might not only render their delicate voices unfit for exercise at present, but hazard the entire loss of them forever.

The only vacation in these schools in the whole year is in autumn, and that for a few days only: during the winter, the boys rise two hours before it is light, from which time they continue their exercise, an hour and a half at dinner excepted, till eight o'clock at night; and this constant perseverance, for a number of years, with genius and good teaching, must produce great musicians.

After dinner I went to the theatre of S. Carlo, to hear Jommelli's new

[11] "A young Englishman who has been four years in the Conservatorio of S. Onofrio." [Burney]

opera rehearsed. There were only two acts finished, but these pleased me much, except the overture, which was short, and rather disappointed me, as I expected more would have been made of the first movement; but as to the songs and accompanied recitatives, there was merit of some kind or other in them all, as I hardly remember one that was so indifferent as not to seize the attention. The subject of the opera was Demophontes; the names of the singers I knew not then, except Aprile, the first man, and Bianchi, the first woman. Aprile has rather a weak and uneven voice, but is constantly steady as to intonation. He has a good person, a good shake, and much taste and expression. La Bianchi has a sweet and elegant toned voice, always perfectly in tune, with an admirable portamento; I never heard anyone sing with more ease; or in a manner so totally free from affectation. The rest of the vocal performers were all above mediocrity: a tenor with both voice and judgment sufficient to engage attention; a very fine contralto; a young man with a soprano voice, whose singing was full of feeling and expression; and a second woman, whose performance was far from despicable. Such performers as these were necessary for the music, which is in a difficult style, more full of instrumental effects than vocal. Sometimes it may be thought rather labored, but it is admirable in the *tout ensemble*, masterly in modulation, and in melody full of new passages.[d] This was the first rehearsal, and the instruments were rough and unsteady, not being as yet certain of the exact time or expression of the movements; but, as far as I was then able to judge, the composition was perfectly suited to the talents of the performers, who, though all good, yet not being of the very first and most exquisite class, were more in want of the assistance of instruments to mark the images, and enforce the passion, which the poetry points out.

The public expectation from this production of Jommelli, if a judgement may be formed from the number of persons who attended this first rehearsal, was very great; for the pit was crowded, and many of the boxes were filled with the families of persons of condition.

The theatre of S. Carlo is a noble and elegant structure: the form is oval, or rather the section of an egg, the end next the stage being cut. There are seven ranges of boxes, sufficient in size to contain ten or twelve persons in each, who sit in chairs, in the same manner as in a private house. In every range there are thirty boxes, except the three lowest ranges, which, by the King's box being taken out of them, are reduced to twenty-nine. In the pit there are fourteen or fifteen rows of seats, which are very roomy and commodious, with leather cushions and stuffed backs, each

---

d Jommelli is now said to write more for the *learned few* than for the *feeling many*.

separated from the other by a broad rest for the elbow: in the middle of the pit there are thirty of these seats in a row.

.   .   .   .   .

Sunday 4. At night I went to the first public representation of Signor Jommelli's opera of *Demofoonte,* in the grand theatre of S. Carlo, where I was honored with a place in Mr. Hamilton's box. It is not easy to imagine or describe the grandeur and magnificence of this spectacle. It being the great festival of St. Charles and the King of Spain's name-day, the court was in grand gala, and the house was not only doubly illuminated, but amazingly crowded with well-dressed company.[e] In the front of each box there is a mirror, three or four feet long by two or three wide, before which are two large wax tapers; these, by reflection, being multiplied, and added to the lights of the stage and to those within the boxes, make the splendor too much for the aching sight. The King and Queen were present. Their majesties have a large box in the front of the house, which contains in height and breadth the space of four other boxes. The stage is of an immense size, and the scenes, dresses, and decorations were extremely magnificent; and I think this theatre superior, in these particulars, as well as in the music, to that of the great French opera at Paris.

But M. de la Lande, after allowing that "the opera in Italy is very well as to music and words," concludes with saying "that it is not, in his opinion, quite so in other respects, and for the following reasons:

"1. There is scarce any machinery in the operas of Italy.[f]

"2. There is not such a multitude of rich and superb dresses as at Paris.

"3. The number and variety of the actors are less.[g]

"4. The choruses are fewer and less labored. And

"5. The union of song and dance is neglected." [h]

To all which objections, a real lover of music would perhaps say, So much the better.

M. de la Lande, however, allows that the hands employed in the orchestra are more numerous and various, but complains that the fine voices in an Italian opera are not only too few, but are too much occupied by the music and its embellishments to attend to declamation and gesture.

With regard to this last charge, it is by no means a just one; for whoever remembers Pertici and Laschi, in the burlettas of London, about twenty

e The fourth of November is likewise celebrated as the name-day of the Queen of Naples and the Prince of Asturias.

f The Italians have long given up those puerile representations of flying gods and goddesses, of which the French are still so fond and so vain.

g If the characters are fewer, the dresses must be so, of course.

h *Voyage d'un François.*

years ago, or has seen the *Buona figliuola* [12] there lately, when Signora Guadagni, Signor Lovatini, and Signor Morigi were in it; or in the serious operas of past times remembers Monticelli, Elisi, Mingotti, Colomba Mattei, Mansoli, or, above all, in the present operas has seen Signor Guadagni, must allow that many of the Italians not only recite well, but are *excellent actors*.

Give to a lover of music an opera in a noble theatre, at least twice as large as that of the French capital, in which the poetry and music are good and the vocal and instrumental parts well performed, and he will deny himself the rest without murmuring; though his ear should be less stunned with choruses, and his eye less dazzled with machinery, dresses, and dances than at Paris.

But to return to the theatre of S. Carlo, which, as a spectacle, surpasses all that poetry or romance have painted: yet with all this, it must be owned that the magnitude of the building and noise of the audience are such, that neither the voices or instruments can be heard distinctly. I was told, however, that on account of the King and Queen being present, the people were much less noisy than on common nights. There was not a hand moved by way of applause during the whole representation, though the audience in general seemed pleased with the music: but, to say the truth, it did not afford me the same delight as at the rehearsal; nor did the singers, though they exerted themselves more, appear to equal advantage: not one of the present voices is sufficiently powerful for such a theatre, when so crowded and so noisy. Signora Bianchi, the first woman, whose sweet voice and simple manner of singing gave me and others so much pleasure at the rehearsal, did not satisfy the Neapolitans, who have been accustomed to the force and brilliancy of a Gabrieli, a Taiber, and a De Amici. There is too much simplicity in her manner for the depraved appetites of these *enfants gâtés*, who are never pleased but when astonished. As to the music, much of the *claire obscure* was lost, and nothing could be heard distinctly but those noisy and furious parts which were meant merely to give *relief* to the rest; the mezzotints and background were generally lost, and indeed little was left but the bold and coarse strokes of the composer's pencil.[13]

·   ·   ·   ·   ·

Wednesday 7. Today I was favored at dinner with the company of Signor Fabio, the first violin of the opera of S. Carlo; he was so obliging and so humble as to bring with him his violin. It is very common in the

12 By Piccinni.
13 Leopold Mozart, in a letter written in Milan on December 22, 1770, says that the opera "failed so miserably that people are even wanting to sub-   stitute another" (*The Letters of Mozart & His Family,* tr. by Emily Anderson [London, 1938], I, 258).

great cities of Italy to see performers of the first eminence carry their own instruments through the streets. This seems a trivial circumstance to mention, yet it strongly marks the difference of manners and characters in two countries not very remote from each other. In Italy, the leader of the first opera in the world carries the instrument of his fame and fortune about him, with as much pride as a soldier does his sword or musket; while, in England, the indignities he would receive from the populace would soon impress his mind with shame for himself and fear for his instrument.

I obtained from Signor Fabio an exact account of the number of hands employed in the great opera orchestra: there are 18 first and 18 second violins, 5 double basses, and but 2 violoncellos; which I think has a bad effect, the double bass being played so coarsely throughout Italy that it produces a sound no more musical than the stroke of a hammer. This performer, who is a fat, good-natured man, by being long accustomed to lead so great a number of hands, has acquired a style of playing which is somewhat rough and inelegant, and consequently more fit for an orchestra than a chamber. He sang, however, several buffo songs very well and accompanied himself on the violin in so masterly a manner as to produce most of the effects of a numerous band. After dinner, he had a second to accompany him in one of Giardini's solos, and in several other things.

I spent this whole evening with Barbella,[14] who now delivered to me all the materials which he had been able to recollect, relative to a history of the Neapolitan conservatorios, as well as anecdotes of the old composers and performers of that school: besides these, I wrote down all the verbal information I could extract from his memory, concerning musical persons and things. During my visit, I heard one of his best scholars play a solo of Giardini's composition very well; he was the most brilliant performer on the violin that I met with at Naples.

And now, having given the reader an account of the musical entertainment I received at Naples, I hope I shall be indulged with the liberty of making a few reflections before I quit this city; which has so long been regarded as the center of harmony, and the fountain from which genius, taste, and learning have flowed to every other part of Europe that even those who have an opportunity of judging for themselves take upon trust the truth of the fact, and give the Neapolitans credit for more than they deserve at present, however they may have been entitled to this celebrity in times past.

M. de la Lande's account of music at Naples is so far from exact, that

---

14 Emanuele Barbella, an Italian composer and violinist, at one time resident in London.

it would incline his reader to suppose one of two things, either that he did not attend to it, or that he had not a very distinguishing ear.

Music [says this author] is in a particular manner the triumph of the Neapolitans; it seems as if the tympanum in this country was more braced, more harmonical, and more sonorous, than in the rest of Europe; the whole nation is vocal, every gesture and inflection of voice of the inhabitants, and even their prosody of syllables in conversation, breathe harmony and music. Hence Naples is the principal source of Italian music, of great composers, and of excellent operas.[1]

I am ready to grant that the Neapolitans have a natural disposition to music; but can by no means allow that they have voices more flexible and a language more harmonious than the inhabitants of the other parts of Italy, as the direct contrary seems true. The singing in the streets is far less pleasing, though more original than elsewhere; and the Neapolitan language is generally said to be the most barbarous jargon among all the different dialects of Italy.[J]

But though the rising generation of Neapolitan musicians cannot be said to possess either taste, delicacy, or expression, yet their compositions, it must be allowed, are excellent with respect to counterpoint and invention, and in their manner of executing them, there is an energy and fire not to be met with perhaps in the whole universe: it is so ardent as to border upon fury; and from this impetuosity of genius, it is common for a Neapolitan composer, in a movement which begins in a mild and sober manner, to set the orchestra in flames before it is finished. Dr. Johnson says that Shakespeare, in tragedy, is always struggling after some occasion to be comic; and the Neapolitans, like high bred horses, are impatient of the rein, and eagerly accelerate their motion to the utmost of their speed. The pathetic and the graceful are seldom attempted in the conservatorios; and those refined and studied graces which not only change but improve passages, and which so few are able to find, are less sought after by the generality of performers at Naples than in any other part of Italy.

---

[1] *Voyage d'un François.* The inaccuracy with which M. de la L. speaks about music and musicians runs through his work. He places Corelli and Galuppi among the Neapolitan composers; whereas it is well known that Corelli was of the Roman school, and he himself says in another place that Galuppi was of the Venetian.

[J] A sufficient proof of the Neapolitan language being only a *patois* or provincial dialect is that it remains merely oral, the natives themselves, who are well educated, never daring to write in it.

11. J. F. Reichardt

Born at Königsberg in 1752, Reichardt began as a student of philosophy and music. He spent the years 1771–1774 traveling in Germany and set down his impressions in his *Reisebriefe* of 1774–1776. In 1775 he became Capellmeister at the court of Frederick the Great, but left this position in 1785 to go to London and Paris; his sympathetic view of the French Revolution undoubtedly had something to do with this. After Frederick's death he returned to Berlin, but was forced to leave again. He died at Halle in 1814.

Reichardt's literary production is a considerable one. He was a man of broad culture who handled his pen with great skill. The books in which he collected his impressions of Germany (1774–1776), Paris (1804–1805), and Vienna (1810) are valued, not only because of the information they contain but also because of their pleasant style.

From the Briefe eines aufmerksamen Reisenden [1]

[*1774*]

FIRST LETTER

TO HERR SCH[RIFTSTELLER] KR[EUZFELD] [2]

BERLIN

SAD AND lonely as is the way to Elysium, the more splendid, the more charming is its aspect. And yet, my friend, were the shade of Homer or Virgil to appear to you in the moment of your first rapture, would you

---

1 Text: The original edition (Frankfort & Leipzig, 1774), 1–31. Reichardt's title ("Letters of an *Attentive* Traveller") is aimed, of course, at Dr. Burney. In his autobiography (H. M. Schletterer, *Johann Friedrich Reichardt* [Augsburg, 1865], I, 140), Reichardt says: "About this time [1772–1773], Bode's translation of Burney's journal of his musical tour made its appearance, and the intensely patriotic citizens of Berlin were offended by the offhand and (as they thought) one-sided way in which Burney had treated their music.

When Nicolai saw that I had this matter very much at heart, he proposed that I should write something against this journal, and not even the compliments on my violin-playing and on my beginnings as a composer which Burney had paid me in his book could make me hesitate to take up the work at once."

2 J. G. Kreuzfeld (1745–1784), Professor of Poetry and Librarian in Königsberg, Reichardt's birthplace.

then continue your stroll through the attractive fields and valleys or would you not rather hasten to the embrace of the blessed spirits? This was my experience too. Scarcely had I arrived in this beautiful royal city,[a] my greedy gaze—which flits from one object to another and wishes to consume everything that meets it—directed toward its many beauties, not yet had I quite thought out one thought, when I learned that the opera was to begin in two hours and that it would be an opera by Hasse. Need I tell you that I thought no longer of beautiful buildings,[b] nor yet of anything else,[c] but, once I had embraced our mutual friend S., I hastened immediately to the opera house? It was almost two hours before the opera was to begin, but these I by no means lost, devoting them to an inspection of the inner arrangements of the beautiful and lofty building. Solemn majesty is the character of this model of the noblest taste in architecture.

All at once I was startled by a warlike sort of music coming down from above; I looked for the musicians at first in the niches built into the sides of the proscenium; they were, however, less poetically situated, standing in the box nearest the stage in the highest gallery. I have always heard it said that music sounds very confused and unharmonious just before a battle—for then fear causes hands and lips to tremble—and such music seemed here to be imitated.[3] It did not last long, however, and there followed a beautiful and fiery symphony by the late Concertmeister Graun,[4] [d]

a The author has here the honor to assure his readers that henceforth he will never again be charmed by any great city, no matter how beautiful it may be. Having seen many great cities and finding in all of them much unhappiness and incurable disorder, he has come to agree with his friend Rousseau that all the splendor and all the amusements of the great cities are as nothing in comparison with a green meadow and a merry harvest dance and that all the art of a thousand artists is as nothing in comparison with the charm of laughing nature. And he who is insensible to this when it is sung by Weisse and Hiller is, in the author's opinion, heartily to be pitied.

b It is true; Berlin has buildings which few of those in other great cities can rival in beauty and taste. The great Schloss, the Opera House, the Catholic Church, St. Peter's, the Zeughaus, and many palaces are models of the noblest, most luxurious, and highest taste.

c The Tiergarten, made up of various sorts of trees and containing within itself little forests of fir, spruce, and oak, groves of beeches, etc., is a special ornament of the city. The Spree, inhabited by swans, flows beside it, reflecting the firs and spruces in its clear waters. Countless hewn-out paths and several reservoirs intensify its beauty and bear witness that art has here proffered a cordial hand to nature. Unfortunately, however, there are also many beauties as yet unexploited which reveal that art, ordinarily so helpful, has had her hands tied. To sum up the great beauties of the Tiergarten in one word, I shall say that it deserves to be celebrated by Ramler. With its cool shadows it would be more grateful to him

for this than is the hero of many of his admirable odes, who would not envy a certain Roman his singer if he but really knew the immortalizer of his own deeds.

d Mr. Burney, in his musical journal, has sinned grievously against this admirable man. He does not find in his symphonies that fire which I, a more careful observer, have found in very few other symphonies; they need, however, to be performed as I have heard them performed by the composer himself. Mr. B. also refuses to allow his violin concertos to be accounted the masterpieces of their kind which they really are. In invention—in the precise point wherein those who know him best admire him most—in invention, he says, he is wholly wanting. Has Mr. B. then heard anything of his works? Actually not. Just as he noted down all his opinions from the words of the first person he met, so presumably this is also something said to him, and said to him by someone envious of this great man. [For Burney's estimate of the brothers Carl Heinrich and Johann Gottlieb Graun, see his Present State of Music in Germany, II, 224–229.—Ed.]

3 Dr. Burney, who was in Berlin from September 28 to October 5, 1772, also speaks of this "warlike sort of music" (The Present State of Music in Germany [London, 1773], II, 99): "Her Majesty is saluted at her entrance into the theatre, and at her departure thence, by two bands of trumpets and kettledrums, placed one on each side of the house, in the upper row of boxes."

4 Carl Heinrich Graun (1701–1759).

of which only the first movement was played. The curtain went up and one saw a most artistic and splendid scene by the master hand of the Turinese artist Signor Gagliari. I did not look at it long, however, for my attention was now claimed by music which wholly distracted me and made me all ears. It was the first opera of Hasse's [5] that I had seen performed, although I was thoroughly familiar with them all through reading the scores and comparing them with those of Graun. To avoid becoming altogether too prolix, I shall not analyze the beauties of the opera here, but shall merely say that it made the most lively impression on me and that I noted, as an indisputable proof of its general effect, that almost every listener had made mental notes of some of the ideas and that on leaving the theater these were being sung by nearly everyone. If a *melody* leaves an impression on one who is not a connoisseur and remains in his memory, this is an unfailing proof that it is *natural* and *unforced*. Such melody is not peculiar to Hasse; Graun and many others have it also. But something I find only in Hasse is this: once an idea has made an impression, one can never forget it. Wherein lies the cause of this? In this, it seems to me: that the idea is so perfectly suited to the point in the action at which it stands and to the person by whom it is sung that, each time we recall it or sing it, it represents to us at the same time the action and the person. By this means, then, the idea is graven deeper and deeper in our hearts with each repetition; after this, who can forget it? I shall now tell you no more about the composition of this great master, for I shall later on attempt to make a *comparison* between him and the immortal Graun.

But how shall I describe to you the charming singing of a Schmeling [e] and a Concialini? [6] Whatever I could tell you would always express most imperfectly the feeling that she inspired in me the first time I heard her. In view of the great compass of her voice, her delicacy, and her dexterity, one can say of her what the author of a beautiful work says of Voltaire: "He is a migrating swallow who neatly and delicately brushes the surface of a broad river, drinking and bathing himself in flight." Her singing,

---

e Mlle. Schmeling, now more correctly Mme. Mara, has improved uncommonly during the five years she has been in Berlin. Her voice, her execution, her acting—all has changed to her great advantage. Her voice, which formerly had a certain clarity bordering almost on the sharp, on the pointed, has now become more mellow and agreeable. To the connoisseurs of instruments I cannot express this better than by saying that, while she had at first the tone of a Stainer violin, she now has more that of a Cremona, although it is not quite this, but rather a beautiful blend of the two which I have for a long time been trying to transmit to my violin and have finally succeeded. In her execution she has formed herself on Concialini and on her husband, both of them perfect Adagio singers. the latter quite as much so on his violon-

cello as the former with his mellow throat. In acting, Porporino and even her husband (who is certainly one of the greatest geniuses) have been the best models for her that she could have; everyone knows this singer's art, while those who have seen Herr Mara function at Prince Heinrich's private performances grant him the title of a perfect actor.

5 His *Arminio*, libretto by G. B. Pasquini, first performed in Dresden, December 7, 1745. The first performance of the revival to which Reichardt refers took place on December 24, 1773.

6 Cf. Burney, *op. cit.*, II, 107–112, 206–208, and 98, for his impressions of Mlle. Schmeling and Concialini.

however, is often expressive and affecting, although she is surpassed in this by Concialini, whose singing is pure melting delicacy. Porporino, who sings a beautiful and unusual contralto, distinguished himself by admirable execution in singing and likewise as a perfect actor, a virtue one seldom meets with among singers, men or women.

The orchestra played very evenly and often with considerable emphasis; one recognizes by the unusual co-ordination of their performance that they are nearly all of them from the school of our great Benda and Graun. But if I am to speak wholly in accordance with my feelings, I found an insufficient precision with respect to forte and piano.

On this point I must explain myself more clearly.

For perfect precision with respect to forte and piano it is not enough to make the ritornellos loud and to play softly from the point where the voice begins. This much was done perfectly here, but one missed the finer shadings of the loud and soft. Both forte and piano are in Adagio very different from what they are in Allegro; the painter, similarly, uses very different degress of light and shade in depicting a sad or gentle situation and in a merry banquet scene or furious battle piece. Each of these shadings has again a special shading as the voice rises and falls. The significance of each movement, the situation of the character, even the natural voice of each singer and the very key of the aria—all these considerations must be most precisely weighed. For this, however, is required the correct and superlatively fine feeling and the untiring industry of a Pisendel,[f] who, to Hasse's great astonishment, never mistook the tempo of an aria and gave himself almost incredible pains to write into all the parts, of every opera and every piece of church music performed under his direction, the forte and piano, their various shadings, and even the single strokes of the bow, so that in the extremely well-chosen orchestra which the court at Dresden had in his time the most perfect order and precision necessarily prevailed.

Of the increasing and diminishing [g] of a long note or of many notes following one on another, which, if I may so express myself, passes through the whole shading of a light or dark color and which in Mannheim is executed in so masterly a fashion—of this I shall not speak here at all, for neither Hasse nor Graun ever employed it. Why not? This I have never been able to account for. But why they never employed the

---

f Pisendel was Concertmeister in Dresden during the time when Hasse was still there.

g It is said that when Jommelli caused this to be heard in Rome for the first time, the audience gradually rose from their seats with the crescendo and did not breathe again until the diminuendo, when they first noticed that they were out of breath. This last effect I have in Mannheim observed myself.

now so fashionable rapid alternations of forte and piano, in which every
other note is either strong or weak—this I can readily explain as due to
their proper feelings or fine taste. Only he whose taste is wholly dulled
and spoiled asks for strong spices in the food he wishes to enjoy. What
sort of taste can that be which takes pleasure in the lifelike portrait of a
sick man who, in a burning fever, makes violent contortions? Yet what
is this musical effect but violent contortions? Would the painter, who
knows that the beauties of nature are the only subject he ought to
represent to us on his canvases and that good taste has banished everything loathsome from the arts—would he treat such a subject? Ought
not the musician, quite as much as the poet and painter, to study
nature and his Ramler and Watteau? In nature he can study man, its
noblest creature, but in our art we have unfortunately no Ramler or
Watteau as yet. Everyone calculates, everyone broods over harmony—
well and good! I readily admit that we can never sufficiently thank a Bach,
a Marpurg, a Kirnberger for their supremely instructive writings. But one
ought also to attend to the chief and final aim of music; one ought also
to investigate its melody, its expression, and above all its effect. We have,
to be sure, excellent practical works of every description, and from these
a Bach, a Schwanenberger, an Agricola, a Homilius, and many others
might derive and, insofar as the diversity of man permits, establish the
most admirable and unfailing rules. How easy this would be for Capellmeister Schwanenberger, whose eight-year stay in Italy provided him
with a store of knowledge and experience without making of him—what
a blessing—a partisan. For thus far neglecting this he deserves to be and
has been punished. For behold, an English gossip comes flying along and
tells us things, most of which do not even deserve to stand in the footnotes
of a good book of this kind; alas for him who, not knowing with whom
he has to deal, may read his forthcoming little history,[h] which threatens
us poor Germans with double punishment! The punishment, I should
think, was already severe enough for the good man. Should it, however,
still be insufficient to set him to writing, we shall have to conceal from
him for the moment that he is one of the best and most agreeable composers of our day and at the same time a complete virtuoso of the clavier.
Perhaps this will stir him to prove to us, from resentment at least, that he
has still other means of eliciting our applause which only his gracious
modesty has prevented him from showing us before. As to you, gentlemen
—you will forgive me if I take you all together—you who seek to win

h Mr. Burney has promised a history of music, which will no doubt consist, as does his journal, of little anecdotes; unfortunately, two translating factories in Germany are already waiting for it.

general acclaim and the applause of the whole nation with a beautiful opera or piece of church music, which, thanks to your prodigal genius, costs you less pains—at first, to be sure, only a small number would thank and honor you in due measure for such a laborious book. But—without too much offense to your excellent works—it would give you far greater assurance of immortality than they do, for these, as has ever been the way with beautiful works, will have to submit to the melancholy fate of fashion, at least for a time. But the passions and feelings of mankind have always been and will always remain the same. And was it not after all from these, gentlemen, that you wished to derive your rules?

Forgive me this digression. I now return again to my letter.

The following week an opera by Graun was given; [7] it had much that was agreeable and attractive, but did not have the same effect as Hasse's, although it was more carefully worked out and still better performed. Herr Agricola, who now supplies the place of the late Capellmeister Graun, had contrived a masterly aria expressly for the voice of Mlle. Schmeling, and for Signor Concialini a superlatively affecting aria had been borrowed from Hasse's setting of the same libretto.[1] [8] In these, both singers revealed their full stature. Several arias composed by the *great and inspired author of the history of Brandenburg* [9] were likewise incorporated in the opera, and among these one gave evidence of great talent.

Why was it, however, that despite all this, the opera had less *effect* than Hasse's?

With Hasse, it seems to me, there was *more boldness and strength in the expression, more variety in the melody, and more sagacity, if less science, in the accompaniment.* Inasmuch as these, in my opinion, are in all of Hasse's dramatic works the characteristics distinguishing him from Graun, they deserve, it would seem, to be investigated more particularly.

If one takes the trouble to place side by side the settings by Hasse and Graun of one and the same libretto, one will find that in the expression of the violent passions, such as pride, hate, anger, fury, despair, and so on, Hasse invariably surpasses Graun, while on the other hand Graun

---

1 It is said, however, that this was done because the King was overly affected by Graun's setting.

7 His *Demofoonte*, first performed in Berlin on January 17, 1746. The first performances of the revival to which Reichardt refers took place during the carnival of 1774.

8 Hasse's *Demofoonte* was first performed in Dresden on February 9, 1748; a single aria, "Padre, perdona," is published in F. A. Gevaert's *Les gloires d'Italie*, I, 94–97.

9 Frederick the Great.

invariably surpasses Hasse in the gentle and affecting. Hasse retains, even in complaint and affliction, a certain lofty energy peculiar to him, and he can never descend to perfectly plain and unaffected lamentation or tenderness. Graun, on the contrary, is in such melodies so simple and so affecting that each affected listener—and who, listening to him, is not affected to the point of tears?—believes that he sings himself and that the personal interest he takes in the affliction of the character is dictating the melody to him. In this appears to be reflected the whole character of these two great men, for all those who have known them long and intimately are agreed that Hasse, in his youth a passionate lover, is at all times vehement and that Graun, on the contrary, was humane and a most loving friend. Hasse has a livelier and more fiery gift for invention; one recognizes in most of his works that, in composing, he is more the actor than Graun and that he enters more actively into the situation of the hero whose pain, whose anger, whose despair he is to translate into sounds. Who does not recognize in the admirable and altogether masterly monologue of Artemisia,[j] at the end of the piece, that the composer himself is tortured here by the extremity of pain, and that he is himself frantic, then complaining, then again frantic, until in the end, already almost out of breath, he invokes the gods in the aria "Rendetemi il mio ben, numi tiranni, etc."? A composer who was not himself an actor, that is, who had not, while writing, experienced the whole action, perhaps even singing and acting it out, would have made of this aria an *aria di bravura.* But in the foregoing recitative it has wholly worn itself out—has exhausted its whole suffering in hurling at the gods every reproach that its utterly unhappy situation could suggest. Hasse, too, works for the theater with a greater zest, while Graun invariably neglected his operas until the last moment, composing them then with the utmost rapidity. Graun, we know, first finished the individual arias, either in his head or at the clavier, and afterwards wrote them out in clear copies without changing a single note; his first score was also the one used at the performances. Having harmony at his command, he could do this the more easily. Hasse, in his scores, often strikes things out. But with what intention? Although it is not at all my purpose to suggest that Hasse is the equal of Graun in theoretical knowledge,[k]

---

j "Sarete paghi alfin, implacabili dei?" In Leipzig, I have often heard Mme. Schröter sing this recitative with such consummate expression that, sensitive singer, she drew from me each time cold shivers and warm tears!

k By how much Graun excels Hasse in harmonic science is evident even from the duets, trios, etc., in his operas. These are the best models we have, and the public cannot sufficiently thank Herr Hartung in Königsberg and Herr Decker in Berlin for having made them more closely acquainted with these masterpieces, an honor to the German nation. It is now up to the public to show that they know how to repay a favor and how to appreciate the excellence of this music. How anxious I am—how anxious every friend and admirer of music must be—that such men should be encouraged to continue with the publication of

he has in any case knowledge enough to work as Graun did. But aside from every composer's having his own individual method,[1] Hasse has always the effect [m] in mind, and to this he devotes himself with tireless energy, sacrificing to it everything, so far as consistent with good taste and correct harmony. To this must also be added innumerable circumstances of their lives, all of which must be exactly inquired into if one would avoid doing Graun an injustice in comparing him to Hasse. For although it is beyond question that both are geniuses, yet in their genius very different, there must also be considered many circumstances disadvantageous to Graun where his dramatic works are concerned. With these I shall acquaint you to the best of my ability.

Hasse became known in Italy almost from his first opera and was soon admired, something which gave him no little encouragement; how much, too, the affection of his present wife, Signora Faustina, at that time one of the first singers in Italy, must have contributed to this later on! When he came to Dresden, he found there perhaps the most magnificent court that then existed in Europe; here he received great remuneration and still greater honor. He worked freely and, unhampered by the taste or will of any person, wrote as he felt and as he wished. Difficulties for the singers and the orchestra he had no reason to avoid, for he could rely on them all. At the same time he had also the proud, stimulating satisfaction of knowing that his works were being performed in Italy and at nearly all the German courts with precisely the same success as at Dresden. Thus he wrote rather for his contemporaries than for his King.

Graun, on the other hand, less generally known, worked only according to the taste of his King; what failed to please him was stricken out, even though it were the best piece in the opera. For, to some extent one-sided and arbitrary in his taste, the King permitted Graun neither liberty nor variety in his operas—qualities which after all are most essential to an agreeable, three-hour entertainment—and, what is still more strange, at all times heartily approved these same qualities in Hasse. As regards the singers and the orchestra, excellent as those at Berlin have been at all

---

outstanding works and that the compositions of a Handel, a Homilius, an Agricola, a Rolle, etc., should thereby become more generally known.

[Four volumes of duets, trios, quintets, and sextets from the operas of Graun, with a few choruses, had been published by Decker and Hartung, of Berlin and Königsberg, in 1773 and 1774.—Ed.]

1 Graun's method would assuredly be uncongenial to Hasse's fiery genius, for when Hasse has at length grasped the central idea of a situation, has read the scene repeatedly, and now, almost without reflecting on it, begins to sing it, surrenders himself to its musical inspiration, and

grasps his pen, the flow of his ideas is far too violent to be as it were measured and divided off in order that harmony may be added to the melody measure by measure and line by line.

m One cannot help being astonished when one hears this admirable man speak about the theater. Never, to my knowledge, has a composer had more experience than he; never has effect been studied more assiduously and with greater success. And this, presumably, is the point distinguishing him above all from every other composer—the point wherein he is the greatest who has ever written. For his slightest works often have more effect than the best and most labored works of others.

times, the greatest connoisseurs who have known them both have always given the preference to those at Dresden, under the direction of Concert-meister Pisendel. What must have been a further heavy blow to Graun was that he saw the operas of Hasse performed at the court of his own King with great applause, often greater than that accorded to his. Yet, despite this, he was in many works obliged to avoid all similarity to Hasse. If now, to all these circumstances, one adds a difference in the genius of these two great men, can one ask any longer why it is that Hasse has more *boldness and fire in his expression?*

But Hasse has also *more variety in melody.* Into this again there enter circumstances which prevent our ascribing, *without qualification,* greater power of invention to Hasse than to Graun. Hasse went often to Italy; there he heard on each visit new works; from these he extracted, as does the busy bee from buds and blossoms, the finest nectar, preparing then from this, as does the bee, a dainty honey which one consumed with pleasure, without concern for the fields and flowers from which it was prepared. For when one looks closely at the operas written and performed in Italy at a given time, one finds whole passages, indeed whole similar movements, which Hasse has used and in using improved. For when he noted in these operas this or that melody, he noted also, and with con-siderable penetration, what was wrong with it; this being corrected, he used the melody in a perfect form, thus making it, so to speak, his own. Graun did not have this good fortune. Almost continuously in *one* spot, he studied, to be sure, the best works, but one knows what a difference there is in music between *hearing* and *reading,* especially with respect to melody, still more especially with respect to effect. By this means Graun could make himself one of the greatest harmonists of our time, and he did so; for theatrical works, however, this helps little more than it helps the landscape painter to have a complete understanding of architecture. Assuredly it gives us pleasure to see a beautiful temple in a background or to see, surmounting a steep crag at whose foot a rushing stream whirls past, the castle of an ancient German prince; if, however, the artist neglects the meadows and valleys, the hills and forests, and the overhang-ing sky, we give him little thanks for his fine buildings, which ought only to stand there as contrasts to laughing nature, but which in this case ob scure it and make it tedious.

To this is to be added still another circumstance. No one can precisely condemn Graun for having neglected his secondary characters, like the painter who places his secondary figures in the shade in order that his principal figure may stand out the more. But one may ask whether, on this account, the secondary characters need all resemble one another. On the other hand, no one can help commending Hasse for having given attractive melodies and some variety even to his secondary characters and for having done this with well-nigh inexhaustible liberality in every aria, always retaining, at the same time, the noble and lofty for his principal characters alone. It is for this reason that, with Hasse, each listener remains continuously attentive and always finds fresh enjoyment, so that the hours slip by for him without his knowing how. With Graun, on the contrary, the so-called amateur often complains of monotony; having no knowledge of harmony—for Graun is always the man for him who has this—he often says, "I have heard this opera before," even though it is being performed for the first time.

Take the score of any one of Hasse's operas, compare it with one by Graun, and you will be persuaded of the truth of all these observations. Then, inasmuch as you have the two scores in hand, look also for a moment at the accompaniment of the voices. In their general style you will find them in this respect almost identical. But at this point observe Hasse's shrewdness. Here, from the very beginning, the two violins proceed in unison. Why is this? To impress the subject on the listener the more effectively. The bass proceeds in notes of larger value; the upper voice is to be clearly heard. "Well, no doubt the viola will so fill things out that at least a closely woven three-part pattern will emerge." So one would think. But look here—it only touches here and there a few notes not present in the upper and lower voices; for the rest it proceeds with the bass. "Well, that must sound very thin." Do you think so? Do you not also know that the composer of operas is in this not very different from the painter of scenery, who must paint everything with great sweeping strokes of his brush in order that, at the distance from which the beholder perceives it, it may for the first time seem to be that which it would represent? Now look for a moment at this aria by Graun. What a fine piece of work! How beautifully the voices imitate one another here! Look at this passage which you liked so much in the ritornello; now the voices have it in three-fold imitation; it is a joy to hear them contending in this way. But we have entirely forgotten the singer! Let us look to him again—heavens, what a face he is making! "Don't you understand it? He is angry that the accompanying voices have more than he has and that they so cover him up that one does not hear him." How did the melody go? Don't you recall it any more? "No—everything has been confused and obscured for me."

In this connection, the story of the two Greek sculptors is in point. Each is asked to make a goddess to be set up in a temple at a considerable height. This being done, the two figures are exhibited to the crowd. Scarcely have they been unveiled when everyone runs to the one figure, shouting: "This is beauty! This is art! With what industry and pains all this is worked out! As to that other one—fie on its distorted face! What a broad high forehead it has! What a nose, and what a big space between it and the mouth! Who ever saw such a face on a goddess?" The shrewder artist is silent and asks only that the two figures be placed in position. His is the first to be elevated. As it rises further and further from the floor it seems to undergo a transformation; astonishment overcomes the crowd and confused mutterings are heard. At length it stands in position, and the crowd grows still, standing as though rooted to the spot, blinded by its beauty. Then the other figure is elevated in its turn. It too is transformed, for no one can any longer recognize it. Its features are confused one with another; although one still perceives the beautiful harmony of its larger proportions, the expression—the soul which had seemed at first to hover about its face—is lost. The one artist recognizes his mistake and disappears, while the other, surrounded by the crowd, is crowned with the triumph, honor, and praise that accompany him for the remainder of his life.

I have attempted here, insofar as the shortness of the time and my insignificant talents permitted, to make a *comparison* between Hasse and Graun in their dramatic works. But you still do not know these men by half, especially Graun. You have seen how many circumstances were unfavorable to him—the lack of opportunity to hear different kinds of music, the sole means by which one can study effect; the confining influence of his King; the want of zest for the theater arising therefrom; the insufficient remuneration and appreciation of his merits—all these and still other private circumstances could not fail to bring it about that Hasse, to whom every circumstance was favorable, should surpass him in this department. Now, however, we shall leave the theater and listen to the two men in the *church*, where nothing is unfavorable to Graun and where indeed his great musical learning is rather an advantage to him. Here for the first time you see Graun in all his greatness. And he who does not admire him here with deep veneration is uninformed, insensible, and prejudiced. To-day, however, I have perhaps already abused your patience; I shall accordingly spare you this voluminous material until another letter. Besides, in a few days I hope to hear Graun's masterpiece.[10] Inspiring me, through this, with ardor for him, he will perhaps himself dictate the words in

---

10 *Der Tod Jesu.*

which I am to sing his praises, I who would not have presumed to pass judgment on him, too far removed from him till now, had nature not given me good instincts and had fortune not led me to a man who, correcting my good instincts, has filled my whole being with love, respect, and gratitude toward him.

12. A. E. M. Grétry

Grétry was born at Liége, Belgium, in 1742. He had little real training. In 1759 he went to Rome, where he stayed for five years without ever settling down to solid work in counterpoint. Eventually Grétry went on to Paris, where at first he met with difficulties; soon, however, his music won favor and he became extraordinarily successful as a composer of comic operas. In the history of French *opéra comique* Grétry is an outstanding figure. Among his many works the following are particularly outstanding: *Le tableau parlant* (1769); *Les deux avares* (1770); *Zémire et Azor* (1771); *La rosière de Salency* (1773); *Colinette à la cour* (1782); *Richard Coeur-de-Lion* (1784)—perhaps his masterpiece; *Raoul Barbe-Bleue* (1789). In his *Mémoires; ou Essais sur la musique* (1789, in one volume, and 1797, in three volumes), Grétry expounds his views on dramatic composition. His influence on the younger generation—Isouard, Boieldieu, Auber—was strong and persistent. He died near Paris in 1813.

From the Mémoires [1]

[*1797*]

JEAN JACQUES ROUSSEAU says that to educate oneself one should travel on foot, enjoying at the same time good health and the delightful sensations which the varied spectacle of nature offers at every moment. I left Rome on the first of January, 1767; I saw nothing on my way; I felt neither pleasure nor pain; I was in a good carriage.

Arriving in Turin, I found there a German baron whom I had known in Rome. He proposed that we should travel together to Geneva. He was

1 The second edition (Paris, 1797), pp. 127–128, 129–134, 136, 140, 142–145, 146–151, 155–172, 429–433.

in a hurry and we set out the next day. When we were out of the city, I wanted to say to him, "Ah, Baron, how delighted I am to——"

He interrupted me and said bluntly, "Sir, I do not talk in a carriage." "Very well," I answered.

At the inn that evening he had a great fire lighted, put on his dressing gown, and came toward me with outstretched arms, saying, "Ah, my dear friend, how glad I am to——"

In my turn I interrupted him to say, dryly, "Sir, I do not talk in inns."

He began to laugh like a madman, and gave me the details of a cruel malady from which he was suffering, and complained bitterly of the Roman fair sex, who, he said, had shown him no indulgence.

*   *   *   *   *

At Geneva I parted company with my baron, consoling myself with the knowledge that I should see Voltaire there. After I had been presented at the best houses by my friend Weiss, I found that I had accepted twenty women as pupils. I had been preceded by a little reputation, and the magistrates allowed me to set a higher price for my lessons than that fixed by the government.

The trade of singing master did not please me, besides fatiguing my chest, but it was necessary for me to prepare for the expense which a stay in Paris involves.

The quarrel between the givers of theatrical performances and their opponents was then at its height. The ambassadors of France, Zurich, and Berne arrived in the capacity of mediators, and the Republic caused a theater to be built to amuse their Excellencies and the rebellious citizens. I heard French comic operas for the first time. *Tom Jones*,[2] the *Maréchal*,[3] and *Rose et Colas* [4] gave me great pleasure after I had become used to hearing French sung, which had at first seemed disagreeable to me.

It also took some little time to accustom me to hearing spoken dialogue and singing in the same piece; [5] nevertheless I already felt that it is im-

2 By François André Danican Philidor (1726–1795), the most famous member of a family prominent in French musical life for over a century. Philidor was a celebrated chess player as well as a composer of genuine talent. It was at the suggestion of Diderot and his circle that Philidor returned from one of his tours as a chess player and devoted himself to composition. *Tom Jones* was first produced at Versailles in 1765 and the next year at the Comédie Italienne.

3 *Le Maréchal ferrant*, a one-act piece also by Philidor, first produced in Paris at the Opéra Comique in 1761.

4 By Pierre Alexandre Monsigny (1729–1817), a native French composer of meager musical training, but who, with Philidor and others, is ranked among the founders of the *opéra comique*. *Rose et Colas* was first heard at the Opéra Comique in 1764. All three comic operas were performed in Geneva for the first time in 1766 where they were produced in the original language by a French company.

5 Like the German Singspiel, French comic opera consisted essentially of spoken declamation and closed arias. This distinguished the *opéra comique* from other varieties of opera played in Paris: the *tragédie lyrique* with its *recitativo accompagnato*, and Italian *opera buffa* with its *recitativo secco*.

possible to make a recitative interesting when the dialogue is not. If the poet wishes to build up or develop a character, he has to provide an exposition and to work out his scenes. In that case what can recitative do? Tire by its montony and slow up the dialogue. It is only the young poets who hurry their scenes in the fear of being too long; the man who has a better knowledge of nature knows that effects are produced only by preparing them and gradually working them up to their highest pitch. So let the stage use spoken dialogue. Let us form at the same time actors who declaim and musicians who sing; otherwise our dramatic works will lose the merit which they have and that which they can further acquire. I should like to set to music a genuine tragedy with spoken dialogue; I imagine that it would produce a greater effect than our operas which are sung from beginning to end.

I soon longed to try my talents upon the French language, and this trial was not useless before dreaming of the capital of France. I asked everywhere for a poem, but, although there are many talented men in Geneva, they were too much occupied with public affairs [6] to give audience to the Muses. I took the course of writing to Voltaire, substantially in these terms:

SIR:

A young musician arriving from Italy and for some time established in Geneva would like to try his feeble talents on a language which you daily enrich with your immortal productions. I vainly request the men of talent of your community to come to the aid of a young man filled with emulation; the Muses have fled before Bellona. They have without doubt taken refuge with you, sir; and I implore your intercession with them, persuaded that if I obtain this grace from you, they will from that moment be favorable to me and will never abandon me.

I am with respect, etc.

Voltaire sent me word by the person who had borne my letter to him that he would not reply in writing because he was ill, and that he would see me at his house as soon as I could come.

I was presented to him the following Sunday by his friend Madame Cramer.[7] How flattered I was by his gracious reception! I sought to excuse myself for the liberty I had taken in writing to him.

"Not at all, sir," said he. "I was enchanted with your letter. I have been told about you a number of times; I wanted to see you. You are a

---

6 At this time Geneva was a refuge for advanced thinkers of the French school. The Helvetic Society, founded in 1762, was an effective force in the spread of progressive ideas.

7 Presumably the wife of Sr. Cramer, Voltaire's Geneva printer.

musician and you have wit! The combination is too rare, sir, for me not to take the liveliest interest in you."

I laughed at the epigram and thanked Voltaire.

"But," said he, "I am old and I hardly know the comic opera which is today the fashion in Paris and for which they are abandoning *Zaïre* and *Mahomet*.[8] Why shouldn't you," he said, addressing Madame Cramer, "write a pretty opera for him to work on until I feel like writing one? For I am not refusing you, sir."

"He has begun something of mine," said the lady to him, "but I am afraid it is bad."

"What is it?"

"*The Cobbler Philosopher.*"

"Ah, it is as if one were to say, 'Fréron the philosopher.' "[9]

.   .   .   .   .

Later on, he said to me that I must hasten to go to Paris. "It is there," said he, "that one takes flight for immortality."

"Ah, sir," said I, "with what ease you speak of immortality. That charming word is as familiar to you as the thing itself."

"As for me," said he, "I would give a hundred years of immortality for a good digestion."

Was he speaking the truth?

.   .   .   .   .

My opera with Madame Cramer made only slow progress, and with works of wit and imagination that is almost always a bad sign. At that time the actors of Geneva were giving the opera of *Isabelle et Gertrude*,[10] which had shortly before been performed at the Italian theater in Paris. The poem pleased, but the music seemed weak. I determined to make my first trial with this poem of Favart.[11] I did not encounter too great difficulty. It is true that I was unaware of the rigidity of the language and

---

8 *Zaïre* (1732), inspired by Shakespeare's *Othello*, and *Mahomet* (1741), two tragedies by Voltaire.

9 Elie Catherine Fréron (1719–1776), a conservative critic of encyclopedic thought who singled out Voltaire for an especially virulent measure of abuse. Voltaire was equally caustic: in a play on words, he alluded to *L'Année littéraire*, a journal published by Fréron, as *L'Ane littéraire;* and his minor but pungent farce, *L'Ecossaise,* is aimed directly at Fréron. By comparison the offhand remark above is mild indeed.

10 *Isabelle et Gertrude, ou Les Sylphes supposés,* a one-act *opéra comique* based on Voltaire's *Gertrude ou l'Education d'une Fille,* mu-

sic by Adolphe Blaise, a bassoonist at the Paris Comédie Italienne, performed in 1–65. According to Clément et Larousse (*Dictionnaire des Opéra,* Paris, 1905), the authors introduced airs by Gluck into their "mince partition." The work was first heard in Geneva during the season of 1766–67.

11 Charles Simon Favart (1710–1792), the most successful comic-opera librettist of the period. The diffusion of his plays throughout Europe is a cultural fact of great social importance; it accounts in considerable measure for the spread of the intellectual tone of the French Enlightenment. Cf. Alfred Iacuzzi, *The European Vogue of Favart,* New York, 1932.

that I wrote florid passages on all the vowels. I did not know that one must wait for some such word as "chain," "flight," "warbling," or "triumph" before indulging in them.[12] I perceived, however, as I worked, that the French language is as capable of accent as any other.

.   .   .   .   .   .

This first French opera had a success that was encouraging to me; the public thronged to it for six performances, and that is a great deal for a small city like Geneva.

One of the musicians of the orchestra, a dancing master, came to me to tell me that the young men of the city, following the Parisian custom, would call me out after the performance.

"I have never seen that done in Italy," said I.

"You will see it here," said he, "and you will be the first composer to have received this honor in our republic."

In spite of my protests, he insisted on teaching me how to make a bow gracefully. At the end of the opera I was in fact repeatedly called out and was obliged to appear and thank the public. My man in the orchestra kept calling to me, "That's not the way . . . no, no, no . . . go on, go on . . ."

"What's the matter with you?" his fellows asked.

"He drives me crazy; I went to his house this morning on purpose to teach him how to present himself to the public nobly. Look; could anybody be more awkward and stupid?"

I felt that it was time to go to Paris. I paid a parting call on Voltaire; I saw him moved by the thought of what might befall me, yet at the same time he seemed to envy me. No doubt I was renewing in his mind the time of his own youth, when he launched upon the artistic career in which one sometimes finds glory along with fortune, but much oftener discouragement followed by despair.

He said to me, "You will not return to Geneva, sir, but I hope to see you again in Paris."

I did not enter that city without an emotion on which I had not counted; it was the natural consequence of the plan which I had formed of not leaving it without having overcome all the obstacles that should oppose my desire to establish my reputation there. This was not the work of a day, for during more than two years, I had, like so many others, to combat the hundred-headed hydra which everywhere opposed my efforts.

Word went to Liége that I had come to Paris to compete with Philidor,

---

12 See above, p. 75.

Duni, and Monsigny. The musicians of Liége blamed my parents for my excessive temerity. This menace did not discourage me; on the contrary it enflamed my emulation, and I said to myself, "If I can gain a place near these three skillful musicians, I shall have the pleasure of surpassing the composers of Liége, who recognize that they are at a great distance from them."

I went twice to the Opéra, fearing that I had deceived myself the first time, but I did not understand French music any the better. They gave Rameau's *Dardanus;* [13] I sat beside a man who was expiring with pleasure, and I was obliged to go out because I was bored to death. Since then I have discovered beauties in Rameau, but at that time I had my head too full of the Italian music and its forms to be able to go back all at once to the music of the preceding century. I felt as if I heard certain Italian airs which had become old-fashioned and whose too familiar turns of phrase my master Casali used sometimes to cite to me as evidence of the progress of his art.[14]

．　．　．　．　．

I went at most four times to the Théâtre des Italiens. I knew their best pieces, and I went only to acquaint myself with the talents and the voices of the actors. The range of Cailleau's voice surprised me.[15] I saw him in the *Nouvelle troupe;* the Actor presents himself as singing alto, tenor, and bass, and actually he could have sung any one of the three equally well. It was this first impression of Cailleau's voice which led me to compose the part of the Huron [16] in too high a register. It will perhaps seem extraordinary that the theater which I frequented assiduously was the Français. I did not wish to write the music of anyone else; for that reason I took good care not to study the music of any of the composers that I have cited. The declamation of the great actors seemed to me the only fitting guide, and I believed that a young musician may be proud to have had that idea, the only one which could lead me to the goal I had set for myself; namely, to be myself, taking as my model beautiful declamation.

13 First produced at the Opéra in 1739; it was followed by a parody at the Comédie Italienne called *Arlequin Dardanus* in which Favart had a hand. The version heard by Grétry was Rameau's second revision of the original score.

14 Giovanni Battista Casali (c. 1715–1792), *maestro di cappella* of San Giovanni in Laterano (Rome) from 1753 to his death. It is a little difficult to take very seriously Grétry's account of his arduous contrapuntal studies with this conservative musician, a follower of the Roman school.

15 Perhaps the leading male singer of French comic opera. "All these talents [other performers of the Comédie Italienne] are eclipsed by that of Cailleau" (*Mémoires secrets*, ed. Bachaumont, I:51, 28 fevrier 1762).

16 The title role of Grétry's first Paris comic opera, *Le Huron.* The libretto was by J. F. Marmontel and it is based on Voltaire's *Ingénu.*

None the less, in order to work, I needed a poem, and to find one I went about knocking at all doors. I neglected no opportunity of forming relations with dramatic authors. If one of them read an opera to me, I made bold to say that I was in a position to undertake it, perhaps to astonish him; but I was put off with pretexts, and I learned without astonishment that some well-known musician had been preferred to me. Philidor and Duni,[17] however, strove in good faith to obtain a poem for me. Men of ability are naturally kind and generous. The educated man observes with so great an interest what it costs a genuine talent to make itself known that even the fear of protecting a rival cannot prevent him from actively favoring it.

At last Philidor announced that he had answered for me and that a poet had consented to confide to me a work designed for him. On the day appointed I hurry to his house; the author reads his work; at each scene my mind is so exalted that I find instantly the motive and the character befitting each number. I pledge my word that the work would not have been my worst. When after long studies the soul takes command with such impetuosity, it does not leave the mind the time to go astray. I found the poem only mediocre and cold, but the flame which burned in me could have warmed it up. I embraced the author; how did he fail to see in my eyes that so beautiful an ardor could not be without value for his success? No, he did not see it, for on the second day following, instead of my receiving the manuscript, Philidor informed me that the author had changed his mind. He was willing, however, to have me work on his poem, provided that I worked with Philidor, if that was agreeable to us both.

"Come now, courage, my friend," said that honest man to me. "I do not fear to join my music to yours."

"For my part, I must fear it," said I, "for if the piece succeeds, it will be by you; if it fails, the public will see only me."

One year later Philidor gave the public his *Jardinier de Sidon,* and it is well known that it had little success.

Some days later I presented myself of my own accord to an actor of the Comédie Italienne; he did not conceal how difficult it would be for me

17 Egidio Romoaldo Duni (1709–1775), Italian *buffa* composer who, upon securing a post at the court of Parma where French taste prevailed, adapted Italian comic opera to the French language. The first of these works, a play by Favart parodying Carlo Goldoni's *Bertoldo, Bertoldino e Cacasenno* (Ciampi's setting had been given by the Bouffons in Paris in 1748), is *Le Caprice amoureux,* and Sonneck has shown that it is a pasticcio from the works of more than a half-dozen other Italian composers. Better known as *Ninette à la cour,* it was most successfully performed at the Comédie Italienne in 1755. Duni's later operas were his own compositions. Although the *opéra comique* can be traced to sources in the late seventeenth century, Duni, Monsigny, and Philidor are rightfully regarded as having defined its shape and style. Grétry's works are a direct issue of their efforts.

to succeed in competition with the three musicians who worked for their theater. He sang to me the entire romance of Monsigny, "Jusques dans la moindre chose, etc."

"There is song, sir," said he, "that is what you need to write, but it is very difficult."

As I left him I was composing melodies for romances which I compared with the melodies of Monsigny.

I made the acquaintance of a young poet, a member of fashionable society, who spent his nights gambling and his days writing verses.[18] I urged him to compose a poem for me as a favor; he promised without hesitation. I paid him thirty visits to encourage him in this good work, and as likable libertines often have a kind heart, he let himself be moved and set to work. The subject he chose was the *Mariages samnites*.[a] I went every morning to inform myself of the state of his health; he read to me what he had written; I wrested it from him scene by scene. I had to wait a long time, but no matter; my eagerness to work gave me a patience which could endure any test.

I knew Suard and the Abbé Arnaud.[19] I had them listen to what I had composed of the *Mariages samnites*. The citizens judged me favorably; the Abbé Arnaud especially applauded me with the enthusiasm of the educated man who has no need of the judgment of others to dare to approve.

If I was flattered by this success, my poet was no less encouraged to finish his piece. The citizens I have mentioned announced me in literary circles, and a few days later I was invited to a dinner given by Count Creutz, at that time the Swedish envoy. I executed the principal scenes of my opera; for the first time I heard my art discussed with infinite intelligence. I was struck by this, for I had observed, during my stay in Rome, that the Italians feel too intensely to reason long. An "O Dio!" and a hand placed over the heart are ordinarily the flattering signs of their approbation. Without doubt, that is saying much; but if in this case one sigh includes a rhetoric, one must agree that it is hardly instructive.

Among the men of letters present at this dinner, I observed that Suard and the Abbé Arnaud discussed music with that genuine feeling which the artist, who has felt everything during his labors, knows so well how to

---

a This piece was not the one with the same title given in 1776, of which I shall speak later.

18 Barnabé Farmian de Rozoy, who also wrote the libretto to Martini's *Henri IV* (1774) and a parody on Anfossi's *L'incognita perseguitata* with music arranged by J. B. Rochefort that was performed at the Opéra (1781).

19 Jean Baptiste Suard (1733–1817) and the Abbé François Arnaud (1721–1784), two critics, who together founded a progressive journal called *Variétés littéraires*. They followed the lead of the Encyclopedists in their aesthetic tendencies.

appreciate. Vernet [20] talked to me as if he had composed music all his life. I saw that he would have been nature's musician if he had not been her painter. After all, what matters the path one takes, whether that of the eyes or of the ears, provided that one reaches the heart?

. . . . .

Everything was going as I wished. It only remained for me to find, in my actors, judges as indulgent as the celebrated men whose approbation I had just obtained. I was seeking the means of having them hear my music when my poet informed me that our piece had been refused. We decided that our work should be recast and arranged for the Opéra, for the comedians, and especially Cailleau, had judged it to be too noble for their theater, and they were right. One month sufficed the poet and myself for this metamorphosis. The patrons of my talent (and in Paris one needs patrons if one is unknown) had spoken of my work to the late Prince de Conti, who ordered Trial, the director of his musicians and of the Opéra,[21] to have the *Mariages samnites* performed in his mansion. I copied out nearly all the parts myself, the state of my fortunes not permitting me to meet the cost of giving them out.

When the day arrived which was to decide my fate, Trial sent me word to come in the morning to the warehouse of the Opéra for the rehearsal of the choruses. At this point a practiced pen would be needed to describe all the hostility that I detected in the expression of the assembled musicians. An icy chill reigned everywhere. If I attempted, during the singing, to reanimate that indolent mass by my voice or my gestures, I heard laughter on all sides, and no one listened to me.

I shuddered still more that evening to see all the French court assembled at Prince de Conti's mansion to judge me. From the overture (which today is in part that of *Sylvain*) to the end of the opera, nothing produced the least effect; the feeling of boredom was so universal that I wanted to go after the first act. A friend held me back. The Abbé Arnaud pressed my hand; he seemed furious.

"You are not being judged this evening," he said. "It seems that all the musicians are leagued together to flay you. But you will survive it; I swear it upon my honor."

The Prince had the extreme kindness to say to me, "I did not find ex-

---

20 Claude Joseph Vernet (1714–1789), a French painter especially known for his marines and for the brilliant light quality he simulated on canvas.
21 Jean Claude Trial (1732–1771), a composer of but modest talents whose four operas are less important than the dance airs in the Italian style which he wrote for his aristocratic employer. He was co-director of the Opéra with Pierre Montan Berton (1727–1780).

actly what your friends had announced to me, but I am distressed that nobody applauded a march which I found charming." It was the one which I afterwards placed in the *Huron.*

I must here do justice to one of my singers, who in the middle of the most soporific rendition, displayed all the energy of a great talent and an honest man. If his role had been more important, or, to put it better, if he alone had sung the whole opera, I should have had a success; but as boredom had already overpowered the audience by the time he began, he was unable to rouse it from its lethargy. This distinguished artist, who beyond doubt had never had a soul base enough to oppose the success of rising talents, is Jélyotte.[22]

*   *   *   *   *

As one may imagine, I did not ask the director Trial whether my opera would be given; the question would have been absurd. The men of letters who were interesting themselves in me, seeing that I was planning to leave Paris, engaged Marmontel [23] to write a poem for me. He came to see me and told me frankly that he had given a piece to the Italians (the *Bergère des Alpes*), and that in spite of its little success, he was about to work on a tale by Voltaire, just published, the *Ingénu, ou Le Huron.*

"You restore me to life," I said, "for I love this charming country where they treat me so badly."

This work was composed, words and music, in less than six weeks. The Swedish envoy, who even after my disaster had declared himself my most zealous partisan, begged Cailleau to come and dine with him to hear a work in which a great role was destined for him; he told me later that he was on the point of refusing the invitation, having already so often compromised himself in the interest of poor works. He accepted only out of regard for the Swedish envoy and for Marmontel. He listened to the first numbers with distrust, but when I sang for him, "Dans quel canton est l'Huronie," he showed the greatest satisfaction. He told us that he would take charge of the whole matter, and that we should be played without delay. "And that," said he, "is the man whose talents I have heard so horribly torn to pieces."

From what I have just said, the young composer will perceive how important it is to leave nothing neglected in his first trial, which will either

---

22 Pierre Jélyotte (1713–1797), the leading French tenor of the period. He was also a chanson composer, wrote a ballet produced at the court, and was an accomplished performer on the guitar.

23 Jean François Marmontel (1723–1799), a member and later perpetual secretary of the Aca-

démie des Beaux-Arts, a *littérateur* and critic as well. He wrote librettos for Piccinni and took his side in the Gluck-Piccinni controversy. Marmontel's *Essai sur les révolutions de la musique en France* (Paris, 1777) is one of the chief documents of the time.

make him known or hold back his progress for several years. A young painter is a hundred times more fortunate. A picture is easily placed in its true perspective, but the rendition of music requires preliminary attentions which are hardly bestowed on a little-known artist.

Cailleau conducted me to Madame La Ruette's,[24] where I found the principal actors gathered. I played alone on the harpsichord all the music of the piece. Some days later we had a rehearsal at the theater. When Cailleau sang the air, "Dans quel canton est l'Huronie," and came to the words, "Messieurs, messieurs, en Huronie . . ." the musicians stopped playing to ask him what he wanted. "I am singing my part," he answered. Laughing at their mistake, they began the number again. The opera was rehearsed with zeal, and I felt my hope of succeeding in Paris revive.

On the day of the first performance I was in such perplexity that it had hardly struck three before I was posted at the corner of the Rue Mauconseil; my gaze was fixed upon the carriages and seemed to be appealing for spectators and asking their indulgence. I did not enter the theater until the first piece had been played, and when I saw that they were about to begin the overture to the *Huron,* I went down to the orchestra. My intention had been to recommend my cause to the first violin, Lebel. I found him ready to give the first stroke of his bow. His eyes were inflamed; his features were so changed as to be hardly recognizable. I withdrew without saying a word, and I was seized by a feeling of gratitude of which I have never lost the remembrance. I have since then obtained his nomination as musician of the King, with a pension of twelve hundred francs.

The public behaved like Cailleau; it listened to the first number with distrust. It believed me to be an Italian because my name ends in *i.* I have since learned that the parterre said, "Now we are going to hear florid passages and *fermate* without end." They were deceived and made amends for their premature judgment. The duet, "Ne vous rebutez pas, etc.," removed their prejudice. Cailleau appeared and made the audience love the engaging Huron, who was long regretted at the Comédie Italienne. Madame La Ruette sang the role of Mademoiselle de Saint-Yves with her always finely restrained sensibility; La Ruette, as Gilotin, displayed his comic pantomime without overemphasis; the excellent actor Clairval,[25] always animated by the desire of being useful to his comrades and to the arts, did not disdain to undertake the small part of the French officer. The success of the piece was indicated at the end of the first act

---

24 A singer at the Comédie Italienne, better known as Vilette before her marriage to La Ruette in 1762.

25 J. B. Clairval, a tenor at the Comédie Italienne. Contemporary accounts speak of a small voice but one of unusual quality.

and confirmed at the end of the second. The authors were called for. Clairval named me, and said that the author of the text was anonymous.

If I have ever passed an agreeable night, it was the one which followed that happy day. My father appeared to me in a dream and held out his arms to me; I rushed toward him with a cry which dissipated the sweet illusion. Dear author of my life, how painful it was for me to think that you would not enjoy my first success! God, who reads the secrets of the heart, knows that the desire to procure for you the comfort which you lacked was the first motive of my ambition. But at the very moment when I was struggling against the storm with some hope of success, when cruel friends explained to my unhappy father how rash my efforts were, when, finally, I was the sole object of his anxiety, and, with a voice almost extinguished, he said, "I shall never see my son again. Will he succeed?" death came to end his long-menaced days, which I was about to make happier.

One of my friends, a painter, came to see me the next day. "I want to show you something that will please you," said he.

"Let's go," said I, "for I am tired of hearing pieces read."

"What, already? No!"

"You see before you a man to whom since this morning five pieces accepted by the Italians have been offered. 'All or nothing' is an adage which holds good especially in Paris. The poets who have honored me with their visits are the ones from whom I had vainly solicited a work."

"Ah!" said my friend. "I had a good laugh in the amphitheater yesterday. I was surrounded by these gentry, and at the end of each number they cried out, 'Ah! he will compose my piece; you will see, gentlemen, the work that I destine for him.' If a singer finished a comic number: 'Ah! I have gaiety in my work, too; bravo! bravo! that's my man!' Finally," continued the painter, "have you accepted any of these gentlemen?"

"No; I told them that Marmontel deserved the preference, because he had been willing to take a risk with me."

I went out with my friend; he led me to a little street behind the Comédie Italienne and stopped me in front of a shop. I read, "The Great Huron, N. Tobacconist." I entered and bought a pound, for I found it, of course, better than anywhere else.

If I was delighted with the success of the *Huron*, I was no less delighted with another event which I had been far from expecting. Could anyone have believed, indeed, that at the time of my arrival in Paris, when I was fruitlessly begging, in that great city, for poems to set to music, and when indeed I had no claim to inspire the Parisians with much confidence, Voltaire would keep the word which he had given and on which I did not dare count, by writing comic operas for me? In truth, he, as well as his niece Madame Denis, had shown great indulgence for the numbers I had performed in his presence at Fernay, but a few detached numbers and the music which I had rewritten for Favart's opera *Isabelle et Gertrude* seemed to me to be insufficient claims to excite the attention of such a man as Voltaire and to merit his encouragement. When, in order to persuade me to come to Paris, he assured me that he would work for me, I believed him to be joking, and I was far from imagining that Voltaire could for some moments relinquish the scepter of Melpomene for the bauble of Momus.

None the less he did so, and amused himself by composing the *Baron d'Otrante* and the *Deux tonneaux*. I received the former while the *Huron* was still being played as a novelty. Voltaire's tale entitled *L'Education d'un prince* furnished him with the subject of the *Baron d'Otrante*. I was directed to present the piece to the Comédie Italienne as the work of a young provincial poet. The subject was judged comic and moral and the details pleasing, but they were unwilling to accept the work unless the author made some changes. What shocked them, perhaps, was that one of the principal roles, that of the Corsair, is written in Italian and all the rest in French. This mixture of the two languages is not rare in their theater in the so-called Italian comedies, but it was a novelty in comic opera, and they were unwilling to hazard it, especially as they had no Italian singer. For all that, they distinctly saw in the *Baron d'Otrante* a talent which could be useful, and they engaged me to induce the anonymous young author to come to Paris. I promised to do my best. One can well believe that the proposal made Voltaire laugh, and that he easily consoled himself for his rejection by the actors. As for myself, I was greatly annoyed by this untoward incident, which made me renounce setting his piece to music, as he on his part renounced comic opera.

The public was not slow in placing me in the rank of the composers worthy of its encouragements; but people conceded me too much or else not enough. They began by denying me the comic genre, although there was an element of comedy in the *Huron*. Others attempted to arrange my songs according to the system of the fundamental bass, and it or I now and then failed to meet the requirements.

"I have tried in vain," said one man to me, "to find the fundamental bass of the horn note in the accompanied recitative of Mademoiselle de

Saint-Yves in the second act. What explanation would you offer me for the progression there from one key to another, with no relation between the harmonies?"

"Here it is," said I. "It is because the Huron, whose accents Mademoiselle de Saint-Yves imagines herself to be hearing, is too far from the place of the scene to know in what key they are singing there."

"And if the fundamental bass cannot justify this deviation?"

"So much the worse for the fundamental bass. But it is none the less true that one cannot sing a duet in thirds when one singer is half a league from the other."

"You have reason on your side, but what of the rule?"

I met my man again some time later; "Let your mind be at rest," said he. "I have found the fundamental bass of your note."

Woe to the artist who, imprisoned by the rules, dares not allow his genius to soar unhampered. Deviations are necessary if he is to express everything; he must know how to depict the sensible man who goes through the door and the madman who leaps through the window.

If you cannot be faithful to the truth except by creating a combination never before used, do not fear to enrich theory by one rule more; other artists will perhaps make more appropriate use of the license which you have allowed yourself and will force the most severe to adopt it. The precept has almost always followed the example. It is, however, only the man familiar with the rule who is sometimes authorized to violate it, because he alone can perceive that in a given case the rule has not sufficed.

Now let us try to see why my music slowly established itself in France, without raising up enthusiastic partisans for me and without exciting puerile disputes such as we have seen. I believe that I owe that advantage to my studies and to the manner which I have adopted.

I heard much discussion of music, and as in most cases I did not agree with anybody, I adopted the policy of keeping still. At the same time I asked myself, Is there no way of satisfying almost everybody? I answered, One must be faithful to the truth in declamation, to which the French are very susceptible. I had remarked that a frightful distortion did not disturb the pleasure of the average auditor at the performances of dramatic music, but that the least false inflection at the Théâtre-Français caused a general murmur. I therefore aimed at truth in declamation; after which I believed that the musician who knew best how to transform it into song would be the most skillful. Yes, it is at the Théâtre-Français, from the lips of the great actors, that declamation, accompanied by theatrical illusions, gives us ineffaceable impressions which the best-analyzed precepts will never replace.

It is there that the musician learns to interrogate the passions, to sound the depths of the human heart, to get a clear idea of all the impulses of the soul. It is in that school that he learns to recognize and to reproduce their true accents, to mark their nuances and their limits. It is therefore useless, I repeat, to describe here the sentiments by whose action we have been struck; if sensibility does not preserve them deep within our soul, if it does not rouse tempests there and restore calm, all description is vain. The cold composer, the man without passions, will never be anything but the servile echo which repeats sounds; and true sensibility, listening to him, will be unmoved.

Persuaded that each interlocutor had his own tone, his own manner, I studied to preserve for each his own character.

I soon perceived that music has resources which declamation, being alone, has not. A girl, for instance, assures her mother that she does not know love, but while she affects indifference by means of a simple and monotonous melody, the orchestra expresses the torment of her amorous heart. Does a fool wish to express his love or his courage? If he is really animated, he must have the accents of passion, but the orchestra, by its monotony, will show us the tip of the donkey's ear. In general, the sentiment must be in the melody; the spirit, the gestures, the expression must be distributed through the accompaniment.

Such were my reflections and my studies. I will not say that the actors whom I found in Paris were more actors than singers, and that I was obliged, for that reason, to adopt the system of musical declamation; no, I shall be more faithful to the truth; I shall say that as the music of Pergolesi had always affected me in livelier fashion than any other music, I followed my instinct, which conformed to that part of the public which even in the enjoyment of its pleasures likes to light its way with the torch of reason. The sex endowed with sensibility furnished my first partisans; the impulsive young men credited me with cheerfulness and finesse; the critical said that my music was eloquent; the elderly partisans of Lully and Rameau found in my melody certain relations to that of their heroes. But while the public may be willing to applaud the efforts of an artist, how far he is from being satisfied with his work! He soon comes to feel that the declamation is lost in vague and pleasing melodies, or that a beautiful melody excludes a complete harmony; that he is always bringing out one part by sacrificing another. He sees, as he works, the source of the different systems and the quarrels to which they give rise; but, oblivious of opinion, he must be guided only by the sentiment which dominates him.

.   .   .   .   .

After my arrival in Paris I gave successively the *Huron, Lucile,* the *Tableau parlant, Sylvain, L'Amitié à l'épreuve,* the *Deux avares, Zémire et Azor,* the *Ami de la maison, Céphale et Procris,* and the *Rosière de Salenci.*[26] It was at that period of my career that the Chevalier Gluck brought us his club of Hercules, with which he laid forever low the old French idol,[27] already weak from the blows given it by the Italian Bouffons and then by Duni, Philidor, and Monsigny.

Beyond doubt we owe much to the Chevalier Gluck for the master-pieces with which he has enriched our theater. To his truly dramatic genius should have been confided the administration of a form of enter-tainment to which he had given a new birth by his immortal productions and of which he would have maintained the order and the vigor by his intelligence and by that transcendence which the superiority of talents confers. It is especially by encouraging men of letters, by having referred to himself the different poems that they compose, that it would be easy for a director like Gluck to employ each musician in his own genre. It often happens that a young composer or performer loses several years, perhaps his whole life, seeking what is suitable for him, whereas he could have been settled in a moment.[b]

I know that it is hard to establish subordination among the subjects who subjugate us by the charm of pleasures, but the small merit of those who command them is often the source of their discouragement.

If nature had endowed Lully with the creative genius of Gluck, how brilliantly would he not have made the Opéra of Paris flourish from its birth, being showered with the personal favor of Louis XIV? But that King, a friend of the useful and consolatory arts, could not make a better choice, since Lully was the first musician of his time. It was he who was permitted to create a Royal Academy of Music, of which he was sole di-rector.

Without doubt the courtiers immediately sought to gain authority over entertainments, a sinister authority, which oftener seduces the lover of the fair sex than the lover of the arts; but what could they do against an artist who, like Molière, had the honor of approaching his master to con-

b See the chapter relating to music in the *Instruction publique,* Vol. 3.

26 Grétry's comic operas produced between the

years 1768 and 1773 and listed in an approxi-mately chronological order.
27 J. B. Lully.

sult him about his pleasures? It is said, I know, that too much jealousy reigns among artists to permit too great power to be confided to any one of them. Vain prejudices, vain lies, used to keep the man of talent out of his true place! The mediocre musician, once he has gained a place by his importunate solicitations and his baseness, will doubtless tremble at the sight of genuine talents, whom he will get rid of by affronts; but choose an artist whose deserved reputation guarantees a noble disinterestedness, whose celebrity, that charming phantom, would repulse envy and cupidity if they dared to tempt him; choose the artist who after numerous successes still loves to prolong his glory by lighting the way of young talents by his experience; choose the man, finally, who has the right to say to the famous man, his equal, "Your genius has known how to open to you, in Italy, a new route to truth; why lose yourself in the brilliant path which you have traced for your rivals by pursuing the genre which you cannot attain? Give up those terrible choruses, those dance tunes, of which nature has not revealed to you the animating power; do not deprive Europe of the touching scenes which you produce without effort."

To another he will say, "You, always correct and proud, who have only an inflexible style which cannot lend itself to the infinite gradations of the passions—you should depict only on a grand scale, upon a text of vague meaning."

Finally, to me Gluck would have said, "Nature has given you the melody suited to the occasion, but this talent was given to you at the expense of a severer and more complicated harmony."

It is only at the cost of efforts that we sometimes succeed in departing from the genre to which we have been called; most commonly one overshoots the mark or one falls short of it; the fault is the same.

It would be revolting to self-respect if ignorance should undertake to use this language, but the truth, presented in interesting fashion by an educated man, has always been well received by genuine talents, especially when the director, in order to fill his place well, has an interest in the successes of others.

13. J. F. Reichardt

From the Briefe geschrieben auf einer Reise nach Wien [1]

[*1810*]

FOR EVERYONE, surely, who can enjoy the good things of life, especially for the artist, perhaps quite especially for the musical artist, Vienna is the richest, happiest, and most agreeable residence in Europe. Vienna has everything that marks a great capital in a quite unusually high degree. It has a great, wealthy, cultivated, art-loving, hospitable, well-mannered, elegant nobility; it has a wealthy, sociable, hospitable middle class and bourgeoisie, as little lacking in cultivated and well-informed gentlemen and gracious families; it has a well-to-do, good-natured, jovial populace. All classes love amusement and good living, and things are so arranged that all classes may find well provided and may enjoy in all convenience and security every amusement that modern society knows and loves.

. . . . .

In the city and in the suburbs five theaters of the most varied sort give performances all the year round. At the two court theaters in the city itself, one sees everything outstanding in the way of grand and comic opera, comedy, and tragedy that Germany produces—and, in some measure, Italy and France as well; the same is true of the great suburban Theater an der Wien, where in addition the great romantic magic operas are given with unusual magnificence. At all three theaters, great pantomimic ballets, heroic and comic, are often given also. Two smaller theaters in the Leopoldstadt and Josephstadt play popular dramas of the jolliest

---

1 Text: The original edition (Amsterdam, 1810), II, 138–139, 143–144, 146–150; I, 161–168, 204–210, 218–222, 254–258, 450–454.

kind. On days when no play is scheduled, all these theaters give great concerts and performances of the most important ancient and modern music for church and concert hall. Aside from this, all winter long there are frequent public concerts, by local and visiting musicians, and excellent quartet and amateur concerts by subscription.

For dancing, Vienna makes the greatest and most varied provisions that any city in the world can boast of. The large and small Redoutensaal, the Apollosaal, the Mehlgrube, the Neue Welt, and countless others are dance halls which offer to all classes the gayest, most elegant, and most convenient resorts. The dance music is everywhere outstanding, the service with everything in the way of food and drink is perfect. And with all these amusements, there prevails the best and most jovial spirit, with never a trace of oppressing distinctions.

. . . . .

Viennese society is, moreover, so rich and so agreeable that, as regards hospitality, good living, freedom, and general merriment, Vienna has no equal in all Europe. He who enjoys the good fortune, in Vienna, of coming to know the societies of the various classes, from the higher nobility down to the petite bourgeoisie, enjoys in the highest degree and in the freest and most agreeable way everything charming, delightful, and satisfying that Europe has to offer. At the same time to have everywhere before one's eyes ladies who are beautiful, cheerful, and merry, who are neither affected nor yet impudently forward, is a pleasure one experiences nowhere in the world to the extent one does in Vienna.

To these countless and inexhaustible attractions of Vienna is further to be reckoned that thousands of strangers from all parts and countries of Europe have residences here and travel constantly back and forth, while some have established themselves with taste and not infrequently on a grand scale and live here in great splendor and hospitality. This applies especially to Russians and Poles, who bring the good sociable spirit with them and amalgamate themselves with the Viennese the more easily. Aside from them, the great Bohemian, Moravian, and Hungarian families, like the Austrians, live regularly all winter long in Vienna, giving it the brilliance and magnificence that make it the great splendid imperial city, for the court itself prefers a retired family life to external pomp and show. Yet the court appears also with great dignity and no little brilliance at the few public festivities which it still maintains. The greatest brilliance consists, however, in the rich background provided by the higher nobility of the crown lands.

In the mild and imperceptible gradations from the higher princely nobility, with an annual income of a million, a half million, or a quarter of a million gulden, to the lesser courtly nobility, with an income of a hundred thousand gulden or over; from thence to the petty new nobility, who not infrequently have and spend as much, if not still more—the bankers and great landowners and manufacturers are included here; and so on through the bourgeoisie proper down to the well-to-do petite bourgeoisie; in the way that all the great public diversions and amusements are enjoyed by all classes without any abrupt divisions or offending distinctions—in these respects, Vienna is again quite alone among the great cities of Europe. If, with respect to the first part of this observation, London shows certain similarities, with respect to the second, it is after all very different. In London, an ordinary citizen does not venture into the parterre of the great Italian opera—the drama of the nobility and the great rich world—without having at least marked himself as an elegant and wealthy gentleman by some outward sign—a fine, expensive ring, or something of the sort—and he can in no way obtain admission to a concert or any other sort of entertainment offered by subscription to the nobility—the Concerts of Ancient Musick, for example—unless he is at least related to the great noble families.

Through the utter banishment of all splendor and affectation in everyday costume, even in the greatest houses and circles, Viennese society has gained still more, and I do not know what one could wish added to it to make it perfectly agreeable.

Thus I had the good fortune to spend in Vienna a whole winter, richer in amusements and pleasures of every kind than any winter I have ever before experienced, for all my good fortune in my many earlier travels. If I have one regret it is that the winter continued severe too long to permit my again enjoying to my heart's content the great public art treasures, which, with the utmost liberality, stand free and open to everyone winter and summer and from which, on my first visit to Vienna, I derived so much pleasure and profit. My own work and the hope of being able to remain in Vienna undisturbed throughout the lovely spring season, so endlessly rich in pleasures here, caused me to put off many things, the more so since the extraordinary hospitality of the highest and most noble as well as greatest and most agreeable houses and families offered me daily so rich a social life.

* * * * *

[November 30, 1808] I have been anxiously awaiting a wholly free and quiet moment to describe faithfully for you a touching scene which

I had with old Haydn. Fräulein von Kurzbeck, whom he loves like a father,[2] and Frau von Pereira, full of admiration for him, as for everything great and beautiful, were my guides. As a fitting overture to the scene, Fräulein von Kurzbeck played for me beforehand on her fortepiano a big and difficult sonata by our late Prince Louis Ferdinand. A pupil of Clementi's, she played it in quite masterly fashion, with delicate expression and equally perfect execution which left nothing whatever to be desired in point of purity and clarity.

In one of the outlying suburbs we had to drive nearly an hour into the remotest alleys and corners. Here, in the small but quite attractive garden house which belongs to him, we found the splendid old man, seated at a table covered with a green cloth. Fully dressed in a simple but neat gray-cloth suit with white buttons and an elegantly groomed and powdered curly wig, he sat there quite stiffly, almost rigid, drawn up close to the table, both hands resting on top of it, not unlike a lifelike wax figure. Fräulein Kurzbeck first explained to him that she would like to introduce me; I was almost afraid he would not know my name, or would perhaps not recall it in this state of apathy, and I was really taken aback and (I may honestly say) ashamed when the old hero opened his eyes wider— they still have an animated sparkle—and said: "Reichardt? A —— man! Where is he?" I had just come in, and with outstretched arms he called to me from across the table: "Dearest Reichardt, do come! I must embrace you!" With that he kissed me, pressing my hand tightly and convulsively, then ran his thin hand three or four times over my cheeks, saying to the others: "What pleases me is that the —— artist also has such a good honest face." I sat down beside him and retained his hand in mine. He looked at me for a time, deeply affected, then added: "Still so fresh! Alas, I have put too great a strain on my powers—already I am altogether a child"— and wept bitter tears. The ladies were about to interrupt in order to spare him. "No, let me go on, children," the dear old man exclaimed; "this does me good; these are in reality tears of joy over the man beside me; he will fare better." I was seldom able to bring forth a friendly word of gratitude and could only fervently kiss his hand.

Frau von Pereira, whom he had at first not recognized with his feeble memory, reminded him in a childlike, playful way of various jokes, and

2 Magdalene von Kurzböck, to whom Haydn dedicated his piano trio in E-flat minor and the Viennese edition of his piano sonata in E-flat (No. 52). Reichardt, who had already met Fräulein von Kurzböck at Baron von Arnsteiner's, has this to say of her (I, 145): "One of the most interesting acquaintances I made was Fräulein von Kurzböck, who was presented to me as the greatest pianist among the ladies of the local musical world, and that is saying a good deal. For a long time I had been hearing about her great talent, and I had just heard about it again in Dresden and Prague; I had thus been looking forward particularly to making her acquaintance. She received me as well and as graciously as if she had been looking forward in the same way to meeting me."

he presently joined her in this style, of which he is said to have always been very fond. With this the ladies thought we ought to leave the weak old man, lest in the end he be too much affected, and we took our farewell. Scarcely had we gotten out the door, however, when he called us back, exclaiming: "After all, I must show Reichardt my treasures too!" At that a servant girl brought in all sorts of beautiful things, some of them quite valuable. The most interesting among them was a rather large flat box which Princess Esterhazy, the wife of the now reigning prince [3]—the son of the prince who was for the greater part of Haydn's life his master— had had made for him after her own express design. It was of black ebony, heavily mounted in gold and ornamented with a gold bas-relief.[4] On the lid had been painted the beautiful affecting scene in the Akademiesaal, which, on the occasion of the last great performance of Haydn's *Schöpfung*, proved a veritable apotheosis for the composer.[5] (Collin recently recited to me a really beautiful descriptive poem on this scene.[6]) In the box lay a magnificent big autograph album, likewise black and gold, signed on the cover by the Princess, most cordially inscribed within by the whole princely family. I should be the first artist to inscribe myself, the old man said, and he would have the book sent to me. The whole box, incidentally, was filled on either side with the most dainty writing things and with all sorts of pleasant and useful instruments of gold and fine English steelwork.

Then he showed me further a great number of gold medals—from the musical society in St. Petersburg, from the Paris concerts, for which he wrote several symphonies expressly, and from many others—also a perfectly magnificent ring from the Russian Czar, a diploma from the National Institute in Paris, another from Vienna, conferring honorary citizenship on him, and many other things of this sort. In them the kind old man seems to live again quite happily.

When after a full hour we took leave in earnest, he detained me alone, holding my hand firmly, and told me, while kissing me repeatedly, that I should visit him at least once a week as long as I remained here. I shall not soil this recital with the little anxious touches of avarice he betrayed, in the midst of treasures he could no longer even use—but they went straight to my heart.

The excellent Beethoven I have also called on, having found him out at

---

3 Marie von Lichtenstein, Princess Esterhazy, wife of Prince Nicholas II.

4 For the later history of this box, see Pohl-Botstiber, *Joseph Haydn*, III (Leipzig, 1927), 258-259.

5 This miniature, by Balthasar Wigand, is reproduced in Karl Geiringer, *Joseph Haydn* (Potsdam, 1932), p. 144. The performance in question had taken place on March 27, 1808, some months before Reichardt's arrival in Vienna.

6 Reprinted in Pohl-Botstiber, *op. cit.*, III, 395-396.

last. People here take so little interest in him that no one was able to tell me his address,[7] and it really cost me considerable trouble to locate him. I found him finally in a great deserted and lonely house. At first he looked almost as gloomy as his surroundings, but presently he grew more cheerful and appeared to take quite as much pleasure in seeing me again as I in seeing him, commenting also, openly and cordially, on many things about which I needed information. His is a powerful nature, outwardly Cyclops-like, but in reality sincere, friendly, and kind. He lives much of the time with a Hungarian Countess Erdödy, who occupies the front part of the great house,[8] but he has broken off completely with Prince Lichnowsky, who lives upstairs and with whom for several years he spent all his time. I wanted also to call on the Prince, who is an old acquaintance, and on his wife, a daughter of the excellent Countess von Thun, to whom I owe the greater part of the amenities of my previous stay in Vienna,[9] but I found neither one at home and soon afterwards learned that the Princess lives in virtually complete retirement.

Salieri, who occupies a fine-looking house of his own, I found sitting with a cloth greatcoat over his clothes and frock coat among the music and musical instruments which quite fill his big room, for he never heats it; he wanted me to put on again my own greatcoat, which I had left in the anteroom, but at the moment I was not so chilled, although I cannot ordinarily be as tough as this coarse Italian nature. He has aged, to be sure, since I last saw him, but for all that is still, as he always was, the quite extraordinarily elegant and adroit Italian gentleman in his physiognomy and manner. He too spoke to me in a friendly and confidential way about many things and characterized for me the singers and orchestras of the various theaters with equal frankness and precision. I took leave of him with a sense of pleasure and gratitude.

. . . . . .

[December 10, 1808] Today I must speak to you about a very fine quartet series that Herr Schuppanzigh, an excellent violinist in the service of Prince von Rasoumowsky, the former Russian envoy to the imperial court, has opened by subscription for the winter. The concerts will take place in a private house every Thursday from twelve to two. Last Thursday we heard the first one; there was as yet no great company in attendance, but what there was consisted entirely of ardent and attentive friends

---

7 Krugerstrasse, 1704.
8 To Countess Erdödy, Beethoven dedicated the piano trios, Opus 70, on one of which he was still

working at the time of Reichardt's call, also the two sonatas, Opus 102, for 'cello and piano.
9 During his travels between 1771 and 1774.

of music, precisely the proper public for this most elegant and most congenial of all musical combinations. Had Haydn given us only the quartet, inspiring other genial artists to follow his example, it would already have been enough to make him a great benefactor of the whole world of music. Difficult as it is to bring this sort of music to perfection in performance—for the whole and each of its single parts are heard in their entirety and satisfy only in the most perfect intonation, ensemble, and blending—it is the first variety to be provided wherever good friends of music meet to play together. And since it is charitably rooted in the human make-up that expectation and capacity as a rule keep more or less in step and go hand in hand, each one takes at least some degree of pleasure in the performance, once he has brought to it all that he can offer it individually or through his immediate background. On this account the exacting connoisseur and critic not infrequently finds such groups working away with great enthusiasm, perfectly at home, when he himself, spurred by his overtrained artistic nature, would like to run away.

Here, however, such was not the case. The quartet is on the whole well balanced, although some say that last year, when Herr Kraft [10] played with them, the balance was better. Herr Schuppanzigh himself has an original, piquant style most appropriate to the humorous quartets of Haydn, Mozart, and Beethoven—or, perhaps more accurately, a product of the capricious manner of performance suited to these masterpieces. He plays the most difficult passages clearly, although not always quite in tune, a consideration to which the local virtuosi seem in general to be superior; he also accents very correctly and significantly, and his cantabile, too, is often quite singing and affecting. He is likewise a good leader for his carefully chosen colleagues, who enter admirably into the spirit of the composer, though he disturbed me often with his accursed fashion, generally introduced here, of beating time with his foot, even when there was no need for it, sometimes out of habit alone, at other times only to reinforce the forte. Generally speaking, one seldom hears a forte here—let alone a fortissimo—without the leader's joining in with his foot. For me this ruins the pure free enjoyment, and every such beat interrupts for me the co-ordinated and perfected performance which it is supposed to help bring about and which I had expected from this public production. At rehearsal, where one must continue practicing and assist oneself by all possible means of direction until the piece goes together perfectly, there one may beat time and even shout as much as one pleases. At the per-

10 The 'cellist Anton Kraft. Reichardt will have heard the quartet with Joseph Linke as 'cellist. Kraft subsequently formed a quartet of his own; Reichardt heard their first concert early in 1809 (I, 368).

formance itself, repose in all things is the chief requirement; all preliminary scaffolding must now disappear altogether, and it is far better to
let a mistake pass without censure, whether actually committed or only
feared, than to try to help matters by using strong measures. Not to
mention that the inexperienced and uninformed listener will probably
not notice the mistake in any case, while the more competent will notice
it no less and be doubly offended. Furthermore, an attentive and con-
scientious colleague ought never to be disconcerted by such shameful
public prompting—it can only disturb his repose and control, on which
above all the perfection of the performance depends; an inattentive and
sluggish colleague ought not to count on so ordinary a means of assistance
and stimulation. Each one must help with all his senses and his entire
attention; he who is incapable of this cannot be trained to it by beating
time.

At this first quartet morning there was performed—besides a very naïve
and charming quartet by Haydn, full of good humor and innocence, and
a more powerful, more elaborate one by Mozart—Beethoven's clear and
beautiful Sextet with wind instruments, which made a fine vigorous
effect.[11] In this a horn player from the orchestra of the Theater an der
Wien gave me quite special pleasure, reminding me, with his beautiful
tone and accurate, positive intonation of the half-tones, of our late excellent Türschmidt.

I shall certainly not willingly neglect this agreeable quartet series, to
which Herr Schuppanzigh has given me a ticket.

A few days later, Beethoven gave me the pleasure of inviting this same
pleasing quartet to Countess von Erdödy's in order that I might hear
something of his new works. He played himself in a brand new trio of
considerable force and originality for fortepiano, violin, and violoncello,
altogether excellent and resolute.[12]

The quartet played further several of his older and extremely difficult
quartets. Herr Schuppanzigh revealed a quite special skill and dexterity
in the performance of these difficult Beethoven compositions, in which
the violin frequently competes with the piano in the execution of the
most difficult keyboard figures, the piano with the violin in singing
tone.

The dear Countess, a touchingly cheerful invalid, with a friend of hers,
a Hungarian lady also, took such keen and enthusiastic pleasure in each
beautiful bold stroke, in each fine well-turned inflection, that the sight of

---

11 Opus 81b, an early work not published until
1810.

12 Probably the trio in D major, Opus 70, No.
1, the first of the pair to be completed.

her did me almost as much good as Beethoven's masterly conceptions and performance. Fortunate artist, who can count on such a listener!

· · · · ·

The Liebhaberkonzerte [18] have begun here for the winter, and the one I have just attended was nearly the death of me, for all that the company was very agreeable. In three rather small rooms, the like of which I have scarcely seen here before, a great crowd of listeners of all classes and an almost equally great one of musicians were so crammed together that I lost both my breath and my hearing. Fortunately, however, I did not also lose my sight, for a part of the company consisted of very attractive fine ladies, some of whom also sang very nicely. But even excellent things by Beethoven, Romberg, Paër, and others could have no effect, since in the narrow space one was quite deafened by the noise of the trumpets, kettle-drums, and wind instruments of all sorts. At the same time I was offered something quite perfect to listen to—something that was also thoroughly appropriate here and for this reason did me the more good. It was a Nea-politan guitarist, who played so well that he recalled to me the good old days of the real lute playing; never have I heard anything so perfect from so imperfect an instrument. Two Italians, with agreeable tenor and bass voices, then sang with him a little French romance, "La Sentinelle": facing the enemy in the moonlight, a soldier stands on guard, confiding to the winds for his sweetheart that he watches, lives, fights, and dies for her alone. The elegant Italian, into the bargain a quite handsome young man, a regular Antinoüs, had very cleverly arranged for the guitar a wholly delightful marchlike melody, enriching it with lively interludes. This was perfectly suited to the room and to the company, which was like-wise enchanted by it and appeared not to notice that the whole agreeable impression was destroyed again by Beethoven's gigantic and overpower-ing overture to Collin's *Coriolanus*. In the narrow rooms, my head and heart were nearly burst with the vigorous blows and crackings which each one strained himself to the utmost in augmenting, for the composer him-self was present. It gave me great pleasure to see the excellent Beethoven not only on hand but much made of, the more so since he has in mind and heart the fatal hypochondriac delusion that everyone here persecutes and despises him. To be sure, his stubborn outward manner may frighten off some of the jolly good-natured Viennese, and many of those who acknowl-

---

18 The orchestra of the Liebhaberkonzerte was made up of amateurs, with a few professional players for the wind instruments.

edge his great talent and merits may perhaps not employ sufficient humanity and delicacy to so offer the sensitive, irritable, distrustful artist the means of enjoying life that he may accept them gladly and also take satisfaction in them as an artist. It often pains me to the quick when I see this altogether excellent and splendid man gloomy and unhappy, although I am at the same time persuaded that it is only in his willful mood of deep discontent that his best and most original works can be produced. Those who are capable of appreciating these works ought never to lose sight of this or to take offense at any of his outward peculiarities or rough corners. Only then are they true, genuine admirers of his.

. . . . .

[December 25, 1808] The past week, during which the theaters were closed, the evenings filled with public concerts and musical performances, caused me no little embarrassment in my ardent resolve to hear everything. This applies particularly to the twenty-second, when the local musicians gave the first of this season's great performances at the Burgtheater for their deserving widows' fund, while on the same day Beethoven also gave at the great suburban theater a concert for his benefit, at which only his own works were played. This last I could not conceivably miss; that morning, accordingly, I accepted with many thanks the kind invitation of Prince von Lobkowitz to join him in his box. There we sat, in the most bitter cold, from half past six until half past ten, and confirmed for ourselves the maxim that one may easily have too much of a good thing, still more of a powerful one. Nevertheless—though many a mishap in performance tried our patience to the limit—I was no more willing to leave before the final conclusion of the concert than was the extremely polite and good-natured Prince, whose box was in the first balcony, quite near the stage, so that the orchestra, with Beethoven conducting in the midst of it, was almost on top of us. Poor Beethoven, who had from this concert his first and only ready profit of the whole year, found considerable hostility and only feeble support in the arrangements and performance. The singers and orchestra were made up of very heterogeneous elements, and it had not even been possible to arrange one full rehearsal of all the pieces on the program, every one of which was filled with the greatest difficulties. How much of the output of this fruitful genius and tireless worker was none the less performed during the four hours will astonish you.

To begin with, a pastoral symphony, or recollections of country life.

First movement: Agreeable impressions awakening in man on arrival in the country. Second movement: Scene by the brook. Third movement: Joyous amusements of the country folk. Fourth movement: Thunder and storm. Fifth movement: Benevolent feelings after the storm, joined with thanks to the Divinity. Each number was a very long and fully worked-out movement, filled with the liveliest images and the most brilliant ideas and figures; as a result, this one pastoral symphony alone lasted longer than an entire court concert is allowed to last with us.

Then followed, as the sixth piece, a long Italian scena,[14] sung by Mlle. Killizky, the beautiful Bohemian with the beautiful voice.[15] That today this pretty child rather shivered than sang could not be taken amiss, in view of the bitter cold; in our box near by, we too were shivering, wrapped in our furs and greatcoats.

Seventh piece: A Gloria, with choruses and solos, whose performance, unfortunately, miscarried altogether.[16]

Eighth piece: A new concerto for fortepiano, terribly difficult, which Beethoven played astonishingly well in the fastest possible tempi.[17] The Adagio, a masterpiece of beautiful sustained melody, he actually sang on his instrument with a deep melancholy feeling which awakened its response in me.

Ninth piece: A great symphony,[18] very elaborate and too long. A cavalier sitting near us reported having observed at the rehearsal that the violoncello part, busily occupied, amounted alone to thirty-four sheets. But the copyists here are quite as expert in spreading things out as are at home our lawyer's clerks and court recorders.

Tenth piece: A Sanctus, again with choruses and solos,[19] unfortunately —like the Gloria—a complete failure in performance.

Eleventh piece: A long fantasy, in which Beethoven revealed his full mastery.

And finally, by way of conclusion, another fantasy, in which the orchestra presently came in and was actually followed at the end by the chorus.[20] This strange idea met with disaster in performance as the result of an orchestral confusion so complete that Beethoven, with the inspired ardor of the artist, thinking no longer of his public or of his surroundings, shouted out that one should stop and begin over again. You can imagine

---

14 "Ah, perfido!" Opus 65.
15 Mlle. Killizky (Josephine Killitschgy), Schuppanzigh's sister-in-law, was a last-minute substitute.
16 From the Mass in C, Opus 86.
17 The Concerto in G, Opus 58.

18 The Symphony in C minor, Opus 67.
19 Again from the Mass in C.
20 The Choral Fantasy, Opus 80, a work subjected to further revision before its publication in 1811.

how I and all his other friends suffered at this. In that moment, indeed, I wished that I had had the courage to leave earlier after all.[21]

.   .   .   .   .

[February 25, 1809] Dear father Haydn I am still unable to see again; as often as we send out word to him, asking after his health and for an appointment agreeable to him, we receive from his people the invariable answer that he is very weak and can see no one. Clementi too is most desirous of seeing him again; since his arrival, he has still to succeed in doing so.[22] I fear that his noble spirit will soon depart from us. Although strictly speaking he has for some years been as good as morally dead for the world,[23] one still fears always the final extinguishing of the divine flame which, throughout a half century, has so magnificently lighted the way for us.

Not without being deeply touched can I recall how one of his first "cassations," as he called his cheery, youthful quartets, gave me my earliest artistic joy and was at the same time the chief display piece of my boyish virtuosity; [24] how his quartets, constantly increasing in inner content and character, offered me the best of nourishment and training as well as the most delightful enjoyment; how, on my many visits to England, and especially in France, his superb symphonies were almost everywhere the greatest and the most beautiful that I heard played; how later on his larger choral works for the church and concert hall brought me the keenest and most varied pleasure; and how, after all this, because of a combination of circumstances, I was never able to meet this hero—this patriarch of music—never able to imprint upon his lips or fatherly hand my ardent thanks for all this instruction and enjoyment—until the utmost weakness of mind and body made this for him, as for me, almost a torture. Nearly and deeply affected, I wrote soon after this into his handsome album a choral setting of these magnificent lines from Goethe's "Euphrosyne": [a]

---

a This is now published in the third number of my *Goethe's Lieder, Oden, Balladen und Romanzen* (Leipzig, 1809).

21 The announcement of this concert in the Wiener Zeitung for December 17 describes the program as consisting entirely of new works, not previously heard in public. With the exception of the scena "Ah, perfido!" and the movements from the Mass in C, which had already been heard in performances away from Vienna, this seems to have been strictly true.

22 Clementi had been in Vienna since the latter part of 1808.

23 In a letter to Breitkopf & Härtel written on June 12, 1799, Haydn himself refers to a falling-off of his mental powers; his last significant work was the "Harmoniemesse," completed during the summer of 1802; his death occurred on May 31, 1809, only a few months after the date of this entry in Reichardt's journal.

24 The quartet in B-flat, Opus 1, No. 1; in his autobiography (Schletterer, *Johann Friedrich Reichardt* [Augsburg, 1865], I, 161) Reichardt tells us that this was his boyhood "show piece."

Cliffs stand firmly based; the water eternally plunges;
    Down from its cloudy cleft foaming and roaring it falls.
Ever the pines are green, and even in winter the copses
    Foster on leafless twigs buds that are hid from the eye.
Each thing arises and passes by law; a wavering fortune
    Governs the life of man, treasure of priceless worth.
Not at the brink of the grave does the father, departing contented,
    Nod farewell to his son, blooming and splendid heir;
Nor is the old man's eye closed always by hand of the younger,
    Willingly parting from light, weak giving place to the strong.
Ah, more often does fate perversely order man's life-days:
    Helpless an old man mourns children and grandsons in vain,
Standing, a desolate tree, round which all shattered the branches
    Lie upon every side, ravaged by tempest of hail.

To this I added, from the bottom of my heart: "Also to see the shell of the spirit that will live on among us forever and that created for us a new life, rich in joys and destined—so long as harmony shall remain the highest expression of the endless—to outlive all posterity; also to see the shell so soon demolished filled my innermost being with that deep melancholy which sprang from the heart of the poet and which, in memory of a solemn, never-to-be-forgotten hour, I dared to set to music. For I regard myself as fortunate in having gazed deeply into the soul-filled eye—in having pressed passionately to my heart and to my lips the loving, consecrating hand."

      •   •   •   •   •

Index